Lectionary Tales For The Pulpit

62 Stories For
Cycle B

John Sumwalt

and

Jo Perry-Sumwalt

CSS Publishing Company, Inc., Lima, Ohio

Scripture quotations are from the *New Revised Standard Version of the Bible*, copyright 1989 by the Division of Christian Education of the National Council of the Churches of Christ in the USA. Used by permission.

Library of Congress Cataloging-in-Publication Data

Sumwalt, John E.
    Lectionary tales for the pulpit. 62 stories for Cycle B / John Sumwalt, Jo Perry-Sumwalt.
      p.   cm.
    Includes bibliographical references and index.
    ISBN 0-7880-0817-X (pbk.)
    1. Lectionary preaching. 2. Storytelling — Religious aspects — Christianity. I. Perry-
Sumwalt, Jo, 1952- II. Title.
BV4235.L43S85   1996
252'.6—dc20   96-10535
                                            CIP

This book is available in the following formats, listed by ISBN:
    0-7880-0817-X   Book
    0-7880-0818-8   IBM 3 1/2
    0-7880-0819-6   Mac
    0-7880-0820-X   Sermon Prep

PRINTED IN U.S.A.

In loving memory of our friends,

Martin Elliott
and
Joyce Hamilton Dosch

Acknowledgments

There are many people whose help and support made this book possible:

— Our deepest gratitude to Kerri Sherwood and Cheryl Kirking for providing original musical compositions for three of the stories

— Our thanks to Dorothy Miller, Dorothy Kraemer, Larry Wasson, Steven Dykstra, and Milenko and Eldina Sunjic for allowing us to share their personal stories; to Rod Perry and Rolf Morck for contributing created stories; to Wayne and Ferne Leighty, Kendall Anderson, Joyce Binder, Laura Nyberg, Patricia Marchant, Jerry Sondreal, Robert and Beata Elliott, Gina Alfonso and Lou Fagas for providing information and criticism which assisted us in the creation of some of the stories

— Special thanks to the family of Laurinda Hampton for permission to share portions of her 1979 Christmas letter; to the congregations of Wesley United Methodist Church, in Kenosha, and Wauwatosa Avenue United Methodist Church, in Wauwatosa, for allowing us to test some of these stories on them; and to our children, Kati and Orrin Sumwalt, for their patience, understanding and enthusiastic support of our writing endeavors.

Contents

Introduction

Telling Stories In Church

There are many different uses for storytelling in church settings. When I stopped to think about it, I was surprised at the number and variety of occasions upon which I have told stories in church. I tell stories frequently in the Children's Moment and in sermons.

Retellings of Bible stories are my first choice for the Children's Moment. I believe it is important for children to hear the Bible's stories over and over again, so they will learn them as they do the *abc*'s and the multiplication tables. Understanding and application will come later. I tell some created stories to the children periodically, like "Fearless Freddie" and "The Mighty Acorn," usually in conjunction with the Biblical themes I am exploring in the sermon.

"One In Need Of Healing" and "Dog Days Of The Soul" are examples of full-length sermons in narrative style, which include the telling of a brief story. "Frog Song" is an example of a longer story which stands on its own as a story sermon. I would only do this kind of sermon once or twice a year. Most often, I tell created stories as the conclusion of the sermon, because I know that stories are usually remembered long after the rest of the sermon is forgotten.

I have also learned that stories are well received in many settings outside of Sunday worship.

Meeting Openers

Next time you are responsible for devotions at the board meeting, or you want to set just the right tone at the committee meeting you've been asked to chair, try telling or reading a story. Select a brief, uncomplicated story with a theme that relates to the purpose

13

of the meeting. A Bible story, a fairy tale, a well-known children's story or a pertinent personal story can help get the meeting off to the right start. If you are expecting some tension or disagreement in the meeting, you may want to select a humorous story: a jack tale, an amusing parable or fable might do the trick. One of my favorite resources for such occasions is *Fables* by Arnold Lobel.

Sunday School

The best way to teach a Bible story in Sunday School is to retell it in your own words and then have the members of the class act it out or take turns telling it back to you. If all you do is read the story to them, you can be sure that they will forget most of it by the following Sunday. It is well worth the time and effort to rehearse the telling of a Bible story before presenting it in class. Start by studying the commentaries in your church library and your Bible Dictionary, so that you will have a good understanding of the setting of the story. Include details about the daily life and culture of the characters in the story. Have members of the class take turns being the storyteller. Sit on the floor in a circle around the teller. Develop a good listening atmosphere. Keep distracting sights and sounds to a minimum. Practice listening skills by having the class repeat or retell what they have heard. Pictures may be helpful for illustrating some Bible stories, but using the imagination is preferable.

Jo sometimes throws in a modern image, something out of a McDonald's commercial or a Disney movie, as a way of helping the children make the transition from their own world to the world of the Bible. These "fantastic fabrications" stick in the children's minds, and with them, the story into which they were inserted.

Church Camp

I first learned to tell stories around the campfire at church camp. Campfires are, of course, the best setting for telling stories. Once children have experienced the wonder of listening to a story as the flames leap up into the night, magically and mysteriously in front of their eyes, they will be hooked on storytelling for life — and they will remember what they have heard long after they go home to their Nintendos and boob tubes. "The Pine Lake Creaker" and "The Unknown Camper" are two examples of stories I created for telling in a camp setting.

An outdoor setting may enhance the telling of some Bible stories. Jesus told many of his parables outdoors. Try to duplicate the original settings of the parables. For example, the Parable of the Sower can be told from a boat on a lake, as Jesus told it, while the children gather around on the shore. "The Mighty Acorn" is a retelling of the Parable of The Mustard Seed. It is one of my favorite outdoor stories. The recipe for this one is simple: one large oak tree, one small acorn, tell story.

Men's Club, Women's Club

What do you do when it is your turn to present a program at the men's club or one of the women's circles in your church? Tell a story. Find out what the theme of the meeting is and tell an appropriate story. If the group has a mission project in a foreign country, you might tell stories from that country. I sometimes use these occasions to try out new stories that I'm working on. I tell the group what I am doing and usually find that they become more sympathetic listeners than they might otherwise have been: willing partners with me in the creative process.

Fun Night or Talent Show

Save your funniest, most crowd-pleasing stories for these occasions. If you don't have one, send us twenty dollars and WE'LL fax you one of ours!

Counseling

There is healing, transforming power in stories. The right story told at the right time in a counseling relationship can be therapeutic. Martin Buber's *Tales of the Hasidim*, Michael Williams' *The Story*

Teller's Companion to the Bible and *Friedman's Fables* by Edwin
Friedman are good resources for healing, spiritual stories.

Benefit Story Concert

Next time you need to raise money for some worthy cause,
invite some of the storytellers in your community to give a benefit
story concert. Publicize it well, take a free will offering, or, if your
storytellers are well-known, sell advance tickets. Jo and I helped
raise $500.00 recently in a benefit concert for Passages, a shelter
and counseling service for battered women in our home county.
Jo's brother Rod, a former alderman of Richland Center and well-
known radio personality, created "Old Granddad" for telling on
that occasion.

Christmas Programs

Last December, I was invited to a small church to tell stories at
their Sunday School Christmas Program. I told some of my own
created Christmas stories along with one of my all-time favorites, "A
Legend For Christmas," adapted by William R. White from "Where
Love Is, God Is" by Leo Tolstoy. On other such occasions, I have told
Martin Bell's "Barrington Bunny" from *The Way of the Wolf* and Luke's
account of the birth of Jesus. This year, I will be telling "Flesh,"
"Waiting For Christmas," and "A Voice In The Wilderness."

Weddings

Wedding homilies are usually brief because the congregation
didn't come to hear the preacher preach, they came to witness a
marriage — and to party at the reception afterwards. However,
they will gladly listen to a story if it is not too long, is engagingly
told, and has something to do with love and marriage. My favorite
story to tell in wedding homilies is "Two Brothers," a Jewish folktale
which is included in *Stories for Telling: A Treasury for Christian
Storytellers* by William R. White.

16

Funerals

Personal stories about the deceased, or favorite stories known to have been told by the deceased, can be appropriately told in funeral eulogies or at informal gatherings before or after the service. I find it helpful, when planning a funeral service, to ask family members to share some of their favorite memories of the departed. I find I hear some of the best stories when I ask, "Did she or he have a sense of humor?" Often people will laugh and then there will follow several funny stories about what their loved one used to say or do that delighted family and friends. This very process is healing; it is a way of celebrating and giving thanks for the life of the loved one. Sometimes I will retell one of these stories, with permission, in the funeral sermon. These kinds of stories are usually received with knowing nods, sometimes laughter and, almost always, healing tears. "Dorothy's Story" was shared at her memorial service, at her request. When I finished reading it, I could tell that her witness had touched every soul present in a powerful way. Dorothy Kraemer's life and witness will never be forgotten because we have her story.

John Sumwalt

Advent 1
Isaiah 64:1-9

Painful Waiting

*O that you would tear open the heavens and come down,
so that the mountains would quake at your presence...
From ages past no one has heard, no ear has perceived,
no eye has seen any God besides you, who works for those
who wait for him. You meet those who gladly do right,
those who remember you in your ways. But you were
angry, and we sinned; because you hid yourself we
transgressed. We have all become like one who is unclean
... There is no one who calls on your name, or attempts to
take hold of you; for you have hidden your face from us,
and have delivered us into the hand of our iniquity. Yet, O
Lord, you are our Father; we are the clay, and you are
our potter; we are all the work of your hand.*

— verses 1, 4-6a, 7-8

*Give ear, O Shepherd of Israel ... Stir up your might, and
come to save us! Restore us, O God; let your face shine,
that we may be saved.*

— Psalm 80:1a, 2-3

*"But in those days, after that suffering ... Then they will
see 'the Son of Man coming in clouds' with great power
and glory."*

— Mark 13:24a, 26

The pain was unbearable!

"Where are you, God?" Lucy prayed. "Don't you know how
much I'm hurting? I don't know if I can go on. Are you there,
God? Show yourself! You have always been with us in the past.
You got us through the Depression when I was a kid. You gave
Sam and me both good jobs after the war. We were able to give our
kids all the things we never had. Can you blame us if we didn't

19

have time to go to church? There was too much to do. I know I should have at least taken the kids, and now none of them will have anything to do with church. Oh, Lord, it hurts! Is this some kind of punishment for my sin?"

This was Lucy's seventh trip to the hospital in two years, and the day after her fourth radiation treatment. She was weary of being sick and discouraged by the constant pain. Nothing seemed to help. The doctors and nurses assured her that she would feel better in time. "The odds are in your favor," they said. But Lucy was beginning to lose hope. It had been three years since the cancer had first been diagnosed. She wanted her life back: to have some feeling of normalcy again — to be able to take care of herself, to laugh with friends, to fix a meal and go for a swim — and to be free of the pain. Each agonizing hour seemed an eternity.

"O God," Lucy prayed, "take me away from all of this. I can't bear it any longer."

Lucy slipped mercifully into the morphine fog which had been her only respite from the pain for months and months. When she came to herself a few hours later, she heard the strains of an old gospel hymn being played on the organ in the chapel down the hall. Lucy surprised herself as she began to hum the familiar tune and then to mouth the long forgotten words:

> *Have thine own way, Lord! Have thine own way!*
> *Thou art the potter; I am the clay.*
> *Mold me and make me after thy will,*
> *While I am waiting, yielded and still.*

> *Have thine own way, Lord! Have thine own way!*
> *Wounded and weary, help me I pray!*
> *Power, all power, surely is thine!*
> *Touch me and heal me, Savior divine.*

Adelaide A. Pollard, "Have Thine Own Way, Lord," *The United Methodist Hymnal* (Nashville: The United Methodist Publishing House, 1989), p. 382.

Advent 2
Isaiah 40:1-11

Preparing the Way

Comfort, O comfort my people, says your God. Speak tenderly to Jerusalem, and cry to her that she has served her term, that her penalty is paid ....

— verses 1-3a

A young director faced his cast and crew, slumped in their auditorium seats before the stage of Green Haven medium security prison for women. The youngest member present was sixteen, the oldest nineteen. All had been convicted and sentenced as adults for gang related shootings, stabbings and killings. Their combined sentences averaged 25 years. Most would be in their mid to late twenties before they were eligible for parole. Some would be middle-aged women.

David Pryor's dream of beginning a prison ministry for young felons through stage productions was off to a rocky start. The girls before him were willing enough to fill their empty time learning parts for a musical production, but most had balked at his insistence on a Bible study. Their sullen presence was their testimony.

"So, what is *Godspell* all about?" he asked. Each of the girls maintained her practiced, detached "I don't care" expression and no one spoke. "Sasha," he added, singling out the girl he had chosen to play the vamp role of Mary Magdelene.

"It's about a bunch of hippie clown-types from the '60s," she muttered.

"Naw," another countered, "it's about a Bible story."

"Okay!" David jumped back in. "So why did somebody write a musical play about a Bible story? Who do all of you cast members represent?"

There were shrugs and grunts of dismissal. "Audra, who do you play?"

"Jesus Christ," the girl said with emphasis, making her reply a curse as well as an answer. David's gaze met her hooded glare evenly.

"Right," he said. "Open your Bibles to page 2 in the back section." After much loud page flipping and grumbling he added, "Okay, Jesus Christ, read what's printed after the big number 3, down through the small number 3."

The exotic-looking girl glared at him again, then pulled off the baseball cap she wore, shook out a mane of dark, wavy hair, and stood in her place. "Matthew, chapter 3, verses 1 through 3," she began clearly, to the snorts and chuckles of approval from the group. "In those days John the Baptist appeared in the wilderness of Judea proclaiming, 'Repent, for the kingdom of heaven has come near.' This is the one of whom the prophet Isaiah spoke when he said, 'The voice of one crying out in the wilderness: Prepare the way of the Lord, make his paths straight.' "

With no comment on the girl's knowledge of biblical structure, David hurried on. "Okay, somebody look up Isaiah 40:1-11." The girl named Shirley, who would play the John the Baptist role, raised her hand lazily, and when called on to read verses 3 through 8, repeated the familiar verse from Matthew and continued, "A voice says, 'Cry out!' and I said, 'What shall I cry?' All people are grass, their constancy like the flower of the field. The grass withers, the flower fades, when the breath of the Lord blows upon it; surely the people are grass. The grass withers, the flower fades; but the word of our God will stand forever."

There was no comment when Shirley finished reading. Most of the girls just stared at David. A few stared off into space.

"What you need to understand," David began, "is that Isaiah was ordered by God to tell the people of Israel that God would take care of them. The thing was, another country had defeated Israel in battle and taken all of the young, important, educated people to be prisoners in their country. They left the old, sick, uneducated people in Israel, and sent their army to run Jerusalem and their people to live there. The enemy army tore down the Jewish temple — their most holy place — and wouldn't let the people follow their religious rules anymore. They made them worship the foreign gods. They broke up families. They took away every bit of the Israelites' identity that they could to make them nobody and nothing."

None of the girls looked at David anymore. This they understood only too well.

"The thing was," he went on in a softer voice, "the Israelite people knew that all of this was their own fault. They hadn't been faithful to God, hadn't kept the laws. They believed they were damned forever.

"But then God sent this prophet, Isaiah, to tell the people God still cared. God would bring them home and they would be God's people again. God forgave them for screwing up.

"You see," he concluded, "the people saw their lives as hopeless. They judged God based on their bad experiences alone, not on how great God is. They ignored the fact that God can do anything, anytime. That's why God gave them the message that they would be saved even though they didn't deserve it. The rules can be suspended whenever God decides. That's called grace.

"Now, the prisoners in that foreign land probably thought Isaiah was nuts, just like you think I am, but God's message is just as true today as it was then. You are not just grass. You will be saved by God, like they were, because God said you would be. Time's up. See you tomorrow."

The shuffling and mumbling of the group making their way toward the exit, where armed guards awaited them, was silenced by one voice.

"When did God say we would be saved?" Audra demanded, standing firmly by her seat and glaring at David.

"Ah," the director answered with a smug smile, "That's what *Godspell* is all about!"

23

A Voice In The Wilderness

"I am the voice of one crying out in the wilderness, 'Make straight the way of the Lord.'"

— verse 23

Margaret told herself that she should feel very pleased with her Christmas preparations. The fresh, perfectly shaped balsam tree was trimmed, the outdoor lights and garlands had been tastefully strung, the house had been lavishly decked with wreaths, holly, tinsel and her ever-growing collection of quaint craft decorations. The Christmas cards had gone out early, along with invitations to all of her closest friends to attend a Christmas Eve dinner. The shopping had been completed and gifts lay beautifully wrapped and beribboned beneath the tree, awaiting the modest protestations and delighted squeals of her children and grandchildren. Everything was ready, just as she had planned it. Now she travelled restlessly to the mall, seeking some elusive, last-minute "perfect touches" and the rush that bustling pre-Christmas crowds always gave her.

It didn't seem quite fair, then, that one song from two ragged-looking street kids should ruin her holiday spirit. They stood near the entrance of the mall, looking underdressed for the weather in their denim jackets and jeans. The girl wore earmuffs, a crocheted scarf and mittens as she played her tambourine, but the boy had merely turned up his collar against the lightly falling snow as he strummed his guitar. Perhaps they expected their enthusiasm to keep them warm.

The song wasn't anything Margaret would have associated with Christmas. Instead of the gentle, quiet strains of "Silent Night," or the old-fashioned beat of "Jingle Bells," it was some rock and roll rhythm. The boy danced about, the bobbing of his head throwing his long, greasy-looking hair into his eyes. He had an earring in his nose. The girl kept time with the jangling beat of the tambourine as they sang together. The guitar case lay open at the players' feet with a sign propped inside that said, "Hoping to go home for the holidays. God bless you for your help." There were a few coins and one or two dollar bills scattered on the tattered red velvet lining, which now sported a dusting of snow. Most passersby ignored them, and the Salvation Army bellringer kept throwing them dirty looks, but they sang on, with youthful energy, that disconcerting tune:

Pre-e-e-pare ye the way of the Lord!
Pre-e-e-pare ye the way of the Lord!

Pre-e-e-pare ye the way of the Lord!
Pre-e-e-pare ye the way of the Lord!

Didn't the mall have policies against panhandling? she wondered as she neared. Where was security? As she passed them, trying not to look them in the eye, and yet looking them over, Margaret noticed how tattered their clothing was. The girl was very obviously pregnant, her denim jacket not nearly coming closed over her large middle. The guitar player was still wearing sandals, and though he had heavy sport socks underneath, one of them had a large hole in the toe.

"Merry Christmas!" the girl said when their eyes accidentally met. Hers had teared from the cold, but she wore a joyful smile. She uttered her greeting at the end of one line in the song, then jumped right back in without missing a beat.

Margaret felt angry as she stepped inside the warm, glass-enclosed entryway. She looked at the lights, tinsel, trees and beautiful displays in the store windows she passed, but she didn't feel the joy they always brought her. Hadn't she just been counting all of her Christmas blessings? She had come here to feel good, and just the opposite had happened. Christmas seemed ruined just when everything was prepared … .

Pre-e-e-pare ye the way of the Lord!

The tune wouldn't leave her head, and when Margaret's eyes finally focused on the display in the window she was staring through, there was a tiny baby in a hay manger in a stable. His very young mother was looking at him in awe, and his father stood guard like a sentinel between him and the world outside the cattle stall.

Pre-e-e-pare ye the way of the Lord!
Pre-e-e-pare ye the way of the Lord!

Margaret turned suddenly and hurried back toward the mall entrance. She was afraid that they had left when she neared the glass-enclosed entry without spotting the couple. But when she reached the door she could see that they had only sat down to rest. The boy had closed the guitar case and seated himself on it, and the girl was perched on his lap, strumming the guitar and singing sweetly:

Away in a manger, no crib for a bed
The little Lord Jesus lay down his sweet head.
The stars in the sky looked down where he lay,
The little Lord Jesus asleep on the hay.

Margaret listened until the girl had finished the song and leaned back in the boy's arms, looking cold and dejected. She stepped out into the swirl of large, graceful snowflakes, stopped before the two and held out her hand.

The young couple's eyes were wide with disbelief. There were two one-hundred dollar bills in Margaret's hand. "Everyone should get to go home for Christmas," Margaret said. "Merry Christmas."

The girl took the bills. This time the tears in her eyes were not from the cold. "Thank you. And God bless you."

"God has," Margaret replied, with tears in her own eyes. "God has."

Advent 4
Luke 1:47-55

Home For Christmas

"... he has scattered the proud in the thoughts of their hearts. He has brought down the powerful from their thrones, and lifted up the lowly; he has filled the hungry with good things, and sent the rich away empty."
— verses 51b-53

There were just three shopping days left until Christmas. Mrs. Prosperous Americana was on her way to the bank to pick up the remainder of her Christmas Club money. She had just parked the minivan and was making her way through the parking lot when she came upon a homeless woman sleeping on a bench along the sidewalk. She recognized her as a woman from her Garden Club whom she had not seen for several years. The last word she had heard was that the woman had lost her husband and ended up in a mental institution. Now here she was living on the street. "Oh, my," Mrs. Americana, thought, "I must do something to help my poor friend." Quickly she reached into her purse and took out a large, thick wallet. She opened it, took out a crisp, new, twenty-dollar bill, and then ever so gently and quietly, so as not to disturb her sleeping friend, tucked it into one of the pockets of the woman's tattered coat.

Mrs. Prosperous Americana smiled as she walked into the bank, thinking how good it felt to help someone in need.

That same day, Mr. Active American Churchman was driving his Jeep Cherokee 4X4 along a dark street in the poorest section of the city, on his way to take his turn serving at the soup kitchen, when he happened to see the same homeless woman sitting in the doorway of an abandoned building. He recognized her as someone he had seen often going through the line at the soup kitchen. He stopped the car, rolled down the window, and asked if she would like to ride along with him. She got in the front seat and they went

27

on to the soup kitchen together, she to eat and he to serve. After the meal, he gave her a ride to a shelter. Mr. Active American Churchman helped her carry her things inside and watched as she was registered for the night, given a foam pad, a small pillow, a warm blanket, and shown a spot in the middle of the floor in a large room where she could sleep next to several other women, a baby and three small children. A number of men were sleeping a few feet away, beyond a row of folding chairs, on the other side of the room.

When the homeless woman was settled for the night, Mr. Active American Churchman got back into his Jeep Cherokee 4X4, drove home to a big house in a much nicer part of the city, and told his wife how good it made him feel to help someone in need.

The following morning at 7:00, when the shelter closed, the homeless woman was back out on the street. She made her usual rounds in the downtown area, collecting aluminum cans and food scraps from the dumpsters behind the stores. By late afternoon she was tired, so she sat down to rest on a bench in the park, across from the YMCA. Just then, Naive Young American Christian, on his way to the Y for his weekly swimming lesson, noticed her sitting on the bench and, recognizing her to be a child of God, sat down beside her and introduced himself. She said her name was Barbara and they began to visit. She told him a little about her life, how she had lost her family and how she had come to live on the street. When Barbara was finished, Young Christian looked her in the eye and said, "Barbara, is there anything I can do to help?" "Why, yes," Barbara said. "I would like very much to go home for Christmas."

Young Christian didn't think to ask Barbara where home was for her. He simply offered his arm and led her up the street toward the house where he lived with his mom and dad. He told her what wonderful Christians his parents were and how happy he knew they would be to have her join them for Christmas in their home.

When they arrived at his house in a very nice part of the city, Young Christian took Barbara into the living room where his mom and dad were decorating a large balsam tree with the family's favorite Christmas ornaments. A fire was blazing on the hearth

28

and the sweet voice of Andy Williams crooned "I'll Be Home For Christmas" from the stereo speakers in the corner. Young Christian introduced Barbara to his mom and dad and told them she had come for Christmas. Mrs. Prosperous Americana and Mr. Active American Churchman were completely taken aback. They didn't know what to say.

———————

Author's Note:

This story appeared in our 1995 book, *Life Stories: A Study In Christian Decision Making*, under the title, "Help For The Homeless." John often adapts the story for telling at Christmas and it is this version that is shared here.

Christmas Eve
Luke 2:1-20

Waiting For Christmas

The shepherds returned, glorifying and praising God for
all they had heard and seen, as it had been told them.
— verse 20

There was once a little girl named Lucinda who couldn't wait for Christmas to come. She was so excited about Christmas that she was about to burst! Lucinda loved everything about Christmas. She loved singing Christmas carols, she loved decorating the tree and sending Christmas cards, she loved shopping and wrapping the presents. But, most of all, she loved unwrapping presents on Christmas morning. She couldn't wait to see what she was going to get.

And one year she didn't wait! She sneaked into the closet where her mom and dad had hidden her presents and she peeked. She unwrapped the presents just enough to see what she was going to get. At first she was very excited, because she liked the presents and she couldn't wait to play with them. But later, she began to feel sad. All of the excitement of waiting was gone. Now she didn't have anything to look forward to on Christmas morning.

That night, at the Christmas Eve service, the little girl listened as the Christmas story was read from the Bible. She knew the story well, and she especially liked the part where the angel told the shepherds about the birth of the baby Jesus. How excited they must have been as they made their way to Bethlehem. Their people had been waiting a long, long time for the Messiah to come. Even though it had taken many years, they had never given up hope. And how special it must have been to see the baby Jesus in the manger, even though the angel told them exactly what they were going to see.

"Maybe that's how it will be for me when I open my presents," the little girl thought, and she began to get excited about Christmas morning all over again.

And when Lucinda opened her presents the next morning, what do you suppose happened? She was surprised! She didn't get *any* of the presents she had peeked at! Her sister got all of those. She had peeked at the wrong presents! What a relief it was, and what a valuable lesson she had learned. She would never, ever even try to peek at her presents again! She would wait patiently, and with great excitement, for Christmas to come. She would wait as long as it took.

Flesh

---

*And the word became flesh and lived among us, and we
have seen his glory, the glory as of a father's only son,
full of grace and truth ....*

— verse 14

Uncle Patrick came to live with us after Gram died, in the fall
of my senior year. I had hoped that the big room behind the stairs,
with its convenient outside entrance, would be mine, but Mom said
I would have to wait. Uncle Patty, as we all called him, needed a
place to live. He was her only brother and my only uncle. Dad had
all sisters in his family. He was reluctant to have Uncle stay with
us, but Mom insisted. "It will only be for a little while," she said,
"until his disability comes through from the government." Uncle
Patty was disabled because of his weight and a chronic heart
condition. To say that he was a big man would be a gross
understatement. Uncle Patty was huge: six foot three, 420 pounds:
a hulking mass of quivering, flabby flesh. The whole house quaked
and creaked whenever he moved about in his room. The mattress
and springs on Gram's big four-poster bed were soon sagging all
the way to the floor. He used to open up his shirt and show us kids
his massive stomach. It looked like an unruly sack of feed when he
picked it up in both hands and let it spill out over his belt. "It's all
paid for," he always said. And then he would laugh, that deep,
gutteral, fat man's laugh that we all came to love so dearly that
year he was with us.

Mom told us that he had always been fat, even as a small child.
She said the kids at school used to taunt him with "fatty, fatty Patty"
and "Pat's so fat he can sit on his own lap." Uncle Patty learned to
shrug it off. He told me one time, during one of our late night

32

walks down by the river, that the first couple of years of high school were the worst, until he came to realize that everyone is handicapped in some way. His was just more obvious than others. He said he made a conscious decision when he was sixteen years old to befriend people who had been hurt as he was hurt and to try in some small way to help them feel better about themselves. That was probably why he was one the most loved persons in town. Uncle Patty was caring and sensitive in a way that didn't draw attention to himself. People just liked him. He had a warmth about him which I now recognize, as I look back with the perspective of some years, as a healing presence. Spirits were lifted whenever he came into a room. You knew that he would say or do something that would be uplifting to everyone. I'm not trying to say that he was the life of the party; Uncle Patty in no way fit the stereotype of the jolly fat man. He was a gentle, nurturing soul, gifted with an exceptional intellect and a discerning perceptivity about the meaning of relationships and events that set him apart from most other men and women of his time. The enormity of his obese frame, which repulsed most people upon first meeting, and caused children to point and stare whenever he went about in public, made no difference whatsoever to those of us who loved him. His physical ugliness was part of his glory. To me he will always be the very incarnation of grace and love.

Uncle Patty was one of the few adults I knew in my late adolescent years who treated me as an equal. He listened seriously to what I had to say. And he didn't spare my feelings if I acted foolishly or said something stupid. He always told me exactly what he thought. To this day, whenever I am in any kind of trouble or wonder what to do in a difficult situation, I ask myself, "What would Uncle Patty think about this?" And then it is almost as if I can hear his voice and see his face through the fog, just as I did when he found me that cold December night, bleeding and half dead along the river road.

I had been at a dance with some friends on the other side of town. Uncle Patty had let me drive his 1949 Chrysler Saratoga Coupe — the silver anniversary model. Oh, what a car that was! Uncle bought it used from the Fuller Brush man, but it was in mint condition. It had a hemi V8 engine, a hydraulically-operated transmission, gyrol fluid drive, hydralizer shock absorbers, and safety level ride. It could go from zero to sixty in ten seconds, and it had fold-back seats. My friends were impressed.

When we arrived at the hall, one of the guys announced that he knew someone who could get us a couple of six-packs. We all chipped in, and after only a few minutes he came back with the beer. We drank a round before we went in to the dance, and we had a couple more each when the band took their break near the end of the evening. I had been warned about drinking and driving, but I thought a couple of beers wouldn't hurt — and it would have been awkward to turn down a drink in front of my friends. I felt fine when we started home: a little tired, but certain that my driving abilities were in no way impaired. I dropped my friends off at their homes and had made the final turn on the river road, just a half-mile from our house, when I suddenly lost control of the car. I have never been exactly sure what happened, whether I was going too fast as I came out of the curve or if I hit a slippery spot in the road. The last thing I remember was the car rolling over the embankment toward the river. I thought, this is it, and then I blacked out. They told me later that I was thrown from the car before it went into the water. I don't know how long I laid there in the snow before Uncle Patty found me. When I came to, he was kneeling over me, saying my name.

"Buzz, are you all right? Are you okay?"

"I don't know," I finally managed to say.

"Well, you're alive at least," he said with some relief in his voice. Then he wrapped me in his coat, picked me up, and carried me all the way to the house. Somehow he was able to get me into the back seat of Dad's old Studebaker without adding to my injuries. Then I must have passed out again. I woke up in the hospital bed a few hours after the surgery. Uncle Patty was there with my folks. They all seemed greatly relieved that I was alive and that I would have no permanent disabilities. Nothing was said about my drinking and driving until I was almost well enough to go home. Dad simply told me that I would have to face the music in court and would likely lose my license until I was 21. He suggested that I take the lumps I had coming and learn from it. No one said anything about the car. I knew how much Uncle Patty loved that big Chrysler. When I offered to pay it off, bit by bit, by working extra hours after school, he shook his head and said, "I'm just glad you're okay." I'll never forget that, but it was what he said and did later that left the biggest impression.

It was on Christmas Day, my last day in the hospital. Uncle Patty got there about an hour before the rest of the family arrived. He said, "Buzz, you know that what you did was inexcusable. Drinking and driving is a sin against the community. You risked not only your own life, and those of your friends, but the life of everyone else who was on the road that night. You could have killed someone, or several people, including yourself. The fact that you didn't makes you no less guilty than a criminal who attempts to murder someone with a gun or a knife. To drink even one drop of alcohol, or to take any other kind of drug that reduces your physical and mental abilities while driving, is inexcusable — but not unforgivable."

Then he smiled at me and said, "If we all got what we deserved, life would be unbearable. I once did exactly the same thing you did. Your dad was with me. No one ever found out about our little accident. But he remembers it as well as I do. And now he and I both are kicking ourselves because we didn't prevent you from making the same mistake. Maybe we all have to learn our own hard lessons."

I have never forgotten what Uncle Patty said to me that day, or what he did just before Mom and Dad and the rest of them came into the room with my Christmas presents. He leaned over the bed, put his big flabby arms around me, drew me in close to his massive frame and hugged me with all of his might. I knew then that everything would be all right.

Author's note:

This story first appeared in *Life Stories: A Study In Christian Decision Making*, by John Sumwalt and Jo Perry-Sumwalt, CSS Publishing Company, Inc., Lima, Ohio, 1995.

Praise The Lord!

---

*Let them praise the name of the Lord, for his name alone
is exalted; his glory is above earth and heaven.*
— verse 13

The Board of Bethlehem Community Church gathered for its monthly meeting with solemn resolve. They were the largest, most prestigious congregation in their region, and with that honor came some serious responsibility. Every other year they hosted the Bishop's Winter Renewal Retreat for forty to fifty area pastors. Bethlehem Church's beautiful facility provided meeting rooms and meals for the specially invited clergy and guest speakers. The details were always impeccably managed. Each retreat closed with the Bishop preaching the Sunday morning sermon for the guests and congregation. Participants left feeling pampered and refreshed.

But this year the Board faced a potentially embarrassing dilemma. In the two years since the last retreat, Mae Ella Grant had joined the church.

Now, Bethlehem Community Church was known for its classic, high-church liturgy. The pastor's preaching style tended to attract the intellectual, professional members of the community. The organist and music director had both taught music at a local private college for years. They had attracted many professional singers and musicians to the sixty-voice choir and chamber orchestra. Mae Ella Grant's first visit to the church had been at Easter the previous year. After the choir's beautiful presentation of Handel's "Hallelujah Chorus," she had spontaneously cried out, "Praise the Lord!" Imagine the congregation's shock!

Most everyone had politely ignored that first, indelicate outburst. But the Grant family returned to worship. During each service she attended, Mae Ella managed to lose control of at least one "Amen!"

or "Halleluia!" or "Praise the Lord!" The difficulty was that she was a perfectly charming person in every other way. When her family joined the church, she took an immediate role in Sunday School, the Social Concerns Committee and the Women's Service Society. She volunteered tirelessly to serve at dinners, help put out mailings, and work at the mealsite for the homeless. Everyone came to know and like her. Many tried, directly or indirectly, in gentle and not-so-gentle ways, to tell her how disturbing her outbursts were to the rest of the congregation. Mae Ella would blush and shake her red curls and apologize. But, with a sparkle in her eyes, she would say that, sometimes, there was no controlling the Holy Spirit!

Well, even the most conservative worshipers became accustomed to the outbursts after a year and a half. They could tolerate some spontaneity, especially when they knew Mae Ella was trying to conform. But what would the Bishop and visiting pastors think? The board was solemn, indeed, as they made their preparations.

Another Bishop's Winter Retreat was carried out as impeccably as always after the beginning of the New Year. With tastefully-chosen Christmas decorations still in place, awaiting the arrival of the magi, forty-five pastors were enveloped in the hospitality of Bethlehem Church. Mae Ella Grant was one of the hardest working volunteers that entire weekend. And on Sunday morning she and her husband, a psychology professor at the University, and their three curly-haired children were in their usual places to hear the Bishop speak. Mae Ella, having been cautioned by her many friends to control herself, was on her best behavior.

The choir's moving rendition of "Lo, How a Rose E'er Blooming" nearly did her in. Mae Ella sat on her hands and bit her lip when they were finished. Then one of the guest speakers from the retreat rose to read the Psalm, and his words and the strength of his southern drawl were a balm on Mae Ella's soul. He read:

> *Praise the Lord! Praise the Lord from the heavens; praise him in the heights! Praise him, all his angels; praise him, all his host! Praise him, sun and moon; praise him, all you shining stars! ... Kings of the earth and all peoples,*

princes and all rulers of the earth! Young men and women
alike, old and young together! Let them praise the name
of the Lord, for his name alone is exalted; his glory is
above earth and heaven ... Praise the Lord!
(verses 1-3, 11-13, 14b)

The echo of his last words had not finished ringing through the carved oak rafters before Mae Ella's hands clapped before her and she shouted in return, "Oh, praise the Lord!"

Just as abruptly as it began, her applause stopped as Mae Ella's hands clapped over her mouth. She sank back in the pew in horror of what she had done. But her husband tapped her shoulder and pointed to the Bishop, who now stood in the pulpit beaming a warm smile in her direction.

"Thank you so much for that testimony to the glory of God," the Bishop said directly to Mae Ella. And as the crimson color began to recede slowly from her face, she listened in awe. The Bishop proceeded to preach an inspiring sermon on the importance of spontaneous praise in worship. In it he endorsed the expression of such praise as a regular part of the worship experience. When he came to the conclusion, the Bishop smiled impishly in Mae Ella's direction and said, "Will you all say 'Amen'?" Mae Ella's lilting voice led the staid congregation in a surprisingly strong Amen!

Epiphany 1
Acts 19:1-7

Jesus Loves Rocky Dumar, Too

*Paul said, "John baptized with the baptism of repentance,
telling people to believe in the one who was to come after
him, that is, in Jesus." On hearing this, they were baptized
in the name of the Lord Jesus.*

— verses 4-5

The new young pastor of Lake Bluff Christian Church had seen
the man on the streets of the town frequently. In the first busy
weeks of his new pastorate, he hadn't taken the time to inquire
about him. But when he discovered that the man sat quietly on the
steps outside the church every Sunday, listening, he was determined
to find out about him.

"Oh, that's Rocky Dumar," the secretary replied when he
inquired on Monday morning. "His mother is a member, but she
hasn't come to church for many years. She's a shut-in now. Rocky
just likes to listen to the music."

"But why doesn't he come inside?" the pastor asked.

"I don't know. I've been here for ten years and I've never seen
him 'in' a worship service. Why don't you ask him?"

The next Sunday, as he took his place at the rear of the sanctuary,
waiting to process behind the choir, the pastor peeked out the door.
There, on the top step, sat Rocky Dumar.

"Good morning, Rocky," the pastor said. There was no surprise
on the round face that turned toward him, just a smile. His narrow
blue eyes and slightly protruding tongue indicated Down's
Syndrome.

"Good morning," Rocky answered softly.

"Why don't you come inside and join us for the service?"

He shook his head. "I can't come in. I'm not baptized."

Although the pastor was surprised and puzzled by Rocky's
response, the opening chords of the processional hymn signaled an

end to their conversation for the moment. "Well, you're welcome to come in any time, Rocky. I'm glad you're here," the pastor said, and turned to enter the service.

It was more than a week before the busy work of settling in allowed the pastor to pursue the puzzle of Rocky Dumar's reluctance to enter the church.

"That's an old, long story," the chair of the parish board said when she was questioned on the subject. "When Rocky was about twelve or thirteen his mother wanted him to be baptized and confirmed, like the other youngsters. There were a lot of strange ideas back then about retarded people. His parents hadn't even tried to have Rocky baptized as a baby, but when she saw how well he turned out, and how much he loved the church services, his mother wanted him to become a member. The pastor and the elders back then refused, saying Rocky could attend the class and be baptized, but he wasn't ever going to understand enough to become a member. They wouldn't allow him to come into a position where he could vote and take communion. Of course, back then women couldn't vote, either! Rocky is two or three years older than me, so this was a ways back. My mother would never have dreamed that I would someday be parish board chair! But there are some here who would still hold onto those old ideas in regard to Rocky."

"What about his mother?"

"Oh, she retained her membership, but she and Rocky stopped coming to worship. She's pretty crippled up with arthritis now, and doesn't get out of the house much, but it was protest over Rocky's not being confirmed that made her stay away. She never let him be baptized, either. That must be where he got the idea that that was why he couldn't come into the church anymore. But Rocky always loved the music. He's come almost every Sunday, all these years. He wears his good bib overalls and sits on the steps to listen to the service, even in winter. But after they refused to confirm him, he's never come in."

The young pastor did a lot more visiting with people on the subject of Rocky. Although he was careful to work it in casually in other conversations, so as not to make it a big deal, rumor began to spread that something was up. Those who disapproved made it known in their subtle ways, but he began to form a plan on how to get Rocky Dumar inside the church. The most vital information came from Rocky's mother and Rocky himself. By spring, just before confirmation time, and after a lot of prayer, the pastor knew what to do.

Many of the older members of the church were surprised when Ella Dumar made her way slowly across the front of the sanctuary from the side door on Confirmation Sunday. An usher helped her into the front pew with the confirmation families. And after the confirmation class rose to stand before the congregation, the pastor looked expectantly toward the rear of the sanctuary and said, "Okay, Rocky, you can come in now."

Rocky Dumar walked down the center aisle of the sanctuary in his good bib overalls, his baseball cap in his hands. He took his place in the confirmation line, his grey hair and size sharply contrasting with the rest of the class. The pastor proceeded to question the students on their catechism, and they answered ... some well, and some not so well. Rocky stood quietly, turning his cap in his hands and waiting.

At last the pastor said, "One member of this new group of confirmands is long overdue for this ceremony. Rocky Dumar received his confirmation training in 1941, but he's been brushing up this last couple of weeks with the rest of this class. Rocky needs to be baptized before he's confirmed, and I want to ask him one question before we proceed."

The pastor motioned Rocky forward and turned him to face the congregation. "Rocky Dumar, what does baptism mean?"

Although his speech was thick and a little slow, Rocky's voice was strong and sure when he answered, "Jesus loves the little children. All the children of the world. Jesus loves Rocky Dumar, too."

Then, with his mother's eyes shining on him in pride, Rocky Dumar was baptized and confirmed as a full member of Lake Bluff Christian Church. And *all* of God's people said, "Amen."

Epiphany 2
1 Corinthians 6:12-20

Greta's Glorious Body

Or do you not know that your body is a temple of the Holy
Spirit within you, which you have from God, and that you
are not your own? For you were bought with a price;
therefore glorify God in your body.

— verses 19-20

Greta Schmidt huffed and puffed her way through the church
hallways toward the Parish Nurse's office. She detested tardiness.
It was bad enough in others, but totally unacceptable in herself. As
it turned out, she had eased her bulk into the largest, sturdiest chair
with two minutes to spare, and it took all of that time for her heart
to stop racing and her breathing to settle back into its normal wheeze.
Another "fat class," Greta sighed to herself.

Weight loss clinics, diet clubs, exercise groups and calorie
counting were nothing new to Greta. She had fought a losing battle
with fat from the time she was a small child.

"My momma was an excellent German cook!" she always
laughed, by way of explanation. "Sauerbraten, wiener schnitzel,
kuchen and stollen, sauerkraut, bratwurst, knockwurst and strudel.
Always so much food! And I *loved* it *so much*! And Momma
always demanded that we EAT! EAT! Is it any wonder I look the
way I do?"

But Greta had paid dearly, her entire life, for her love of food.
The other children had teased her and called her names; adults
clucked their tongues and whispered as they stared. She was never
chosen to play games or to be on prom court. No boy ever asked
her out ... ever.

Still, Greta's family life was close-knit and comforting — and
there was the food! She completed high school, attended college
and became a librarian. She lived at home, learning to cook all of

42

her mother's best dishes. As the years passed, Greta cared for her parents, and then her older brother, until, one by one, they went on to be with God. Now, in middle age, Greta's own health had become affected by her food obsession.

"The doctor says I have hypertension, heart problems, gout, and adult-onset diabetes," Greta said in answer to Nurse Betty Anderson's request for all the group members to state why they had come to her class on Wholistic Lifestyle Management. "I've tried every kind of diet on the market. I figure one more can't hurt."

Others in the class shared Greta's health concerns, and more besides, but she noted that few shared her girth. The next largest person present was a man who probably weighed around 250 pounds. Greta couldn't remember when she had weighed that little.

"Would someone volunteer to begin with some scripture readings?" Nurse Betty asked, passing around sheets of paper with several printed texts. A man named Max raised his hand and read:

> *So God created humankind in his image, in the image of God he created them; male and female he created them ... God saw everything that he had made, and indeed, it was very good.*
> — Genesis 1:27, 31

> *When I look at your heavens, the work of your fingers, the moon and the stars that you have established; what are human beings that you are mindful of them, mortals that you care for them? Yet you have made them a little lower than God, and crowned them with glory and honor.*
> — Psalm 8:3-5

> *Yet it was you who took me from the womb; you kept me safe on my mother's breast. On you I was cast from my birth, and since my mother bore me you have been my God.*
> — Psalm 22:9-10

> *Know that the Lord is God. It is he that made us, and we are his; we are his people, and the sheep of his pasture.*
> — Psalm 100:3

43

Bless the Lord, O my soul, and do not forget all his benefits
— who forgives all your iniquity, who heals all your
diseases, who redeems your life from the Pit ....
— Psalm 103:2-4

"Now, tell me," the nurse said, "what theme you hear running through these scriptures?"

"That God made us and we are good," said one woman who was wearing an oxygen mask.

"That we belong to God," said another.

"That God heals our diseases," said Max.

"I want to suggest," Nurse Betty continued, "that this class on Wholistic Lifestyle Management is the beginning of thinking of ourselves in a new way. Jesus said to love God and love your neighbor as yourself. But we can't love our neighbors the way we should if we don't love ourselves! And if we love ourselves, we won't want to put harmful things like cigarette smoke, fatty foods, too much refined sugar and harmful chemicals into our bodies. We need to take care of our bodies through exercise, good nutrition, daily prayer and meditation.

"I'd like to lift up a portion of Paul's advice to the Corinthians as God's advice to us:

> *"All things are lawful for me," but not all things are beneficial. "All things are lawful for me," but I will not be dominated by anything ... Or do you not know that your body is a temple of the Holy Spirit within you, which you have from God, and that you are not your own? For you were bought with a price; therefore, glorify God in your body.*   — 1 Corinthians 6:12, 19-20

Greta huffed and puffed her way back to her car, lost in thought. *Never* had *anyone* told her that her body was special. *Never* had she considered that the food she so loved to eat was a substitute for love and acceptance.

Was that why all the other diets and exercise programs had failed? ... because she had never loved herself — her own body — enough to care for it?

"Let me start over again, God," she wheezed as she squeezed herself behind the steering wheel of her large car. "Help me to love myself enough to glorify you in my body."

Sutton's Folly

*I mean, brothers and sisters, the appointed time has grown
short; from now on, let even those who have wives be as
though they had none, and those who mourn as though
they were not mourning, and those who rejoice as though
they were not rejoicing, and those who buy as though they
had no possessions, and those who deal with the world as
though they had no dealings with it. For the present form
of this world is passing away.*

— verses 29-31

Ed Weeks couldn't believe his bad luck. After seventeen years
of investigative reporting, he had finally gotten his big chance at
an exclusive story. The contacts had all been there, his snooping
had paid off, and what did it land him? Trouble, that was what.
Heart-rending, life-changing trouble.

It had all begun almost eight years earlier when his best buddy
and co-worker, Alan Sutton, hit the big one in the lottery. Al was
one of those dreamers who believed that the only thing standing
between him and total happiness and success was a winning lottery
number. He always said that there was no problem, no ailment, no
misery that money couldn't remedy. And, although most everyone
else at *The Times* agreed, Ed had laughed at him. Ed had been
raised to believe that it was how you lived and treated others, not
how much cash you had, that gave value to your life. And he still
believed that, even though Al Sutton tried to prove him wrong.

Al hit the jackpot just before Christmas, 1988. His ticket took
the whole pot — 28 million dollars. There had been one great
Christmas and New Year's Eve party at the Press Club that year!
In fact, Ed couldn't remember any break in between. The Christmas
party had just kind of "rolled over" into New Year's. Al believed in
sharing the wealth, so all of his buddies benefitted. Of course, he

left the paper. He lived the good life for 4 or 5 years, became a jetsetter. Ed got a kick out of dropping stories for the wire service with shots of Al and beautiful starlets, wealthy business and entertainment moguls, and politicians. And Al was not only good at sharing the wealth, he made more, too. Ed figured that by 1993 Al was worth about $50 million.

It occurred to Ed that Al might have been right after all. Given enough money, the world began to look like a better place. Even though it wasn't for Ed, wealth didn't seem to be doing Al any harm. Then one day, in March of 1993, Alan Sutton disappeared.

There hadn't been any warning. Ed had spoken with Al a few days before about a story he was doing on campaign corruption: politics had always been Al's forte. Al had sounded tired, said he had a bad cold, but there was no indication of trouble. Two days later he was gone. Ed jumped right into the search. In fact, he stayed at it longer than anyone, even the rest of the gang from *The Times*. And before he gave it up, he laid some pretty careful information networks. If Al Sutton surfaced anywhere, Ed Weeks was most likely the first reporter who would hear about it.

But a year passed, and then two, and there was no sign of the person or wealth of Alan Sutton. Ed couldn't believe that he had done "a Howard Hughes," but there was no other explanation. Al Sutton had disappeared because he wanted to, and he'd covered his trail well. Ed Weeks put the search aside, but he didn't forget.

Then, in late September, 1995, Ed got a phone call from a doctor. He said Ed had better get over to an old storefront building on East 72nd Street. He didn't have to say more.

The building was a homeless shelter. It wasn't fancy, by any means, but it was clean and in good repair. The director said the owner had financed everything — repairs, furnishings, paint, food, utilities and medical care — for the past two years. There were 200 beds in the entire building, and they were full almost every night. There was a hot meal in the evening and a simple breakfast every morning. The owner lived on the 15th floor and no one was allowed up there except the director and the doctor. That morning the director had found the owner near death and called the doctor, who had called Ed. Ed asked to go up.

The room was clean and warm, but barren, as were all of the rooms Ed had seen downstairs, although this one had a hospital bed and a lot of medical equipment. The man on the bed was not much more than a skeleton, with angry-looking sores on his face and hands. Ed had no trouble recognizing him as Alan Sutton, though. His hands rested on a Bible that lay open on his chest. When he could make himself move, Ed stepped up to the bedside and looked down at what was left of his friend.

"Thanks for coming, Ed," the skeleton man whispered. "I didn't want anyone to see me this way, but I had to tell you. Not much time left. Had to tell you that you were right."

"Take it easy, Al. There's no rush. I'll stay right here until you've told me what you want me to hear."

Sutton's breathing wheezed shrilly. "Had to tell you that you were right. Money can't solve every problem. I wanted you to know ... and need your help."

"Tell me what you want me to do, Al," Ed said. As a war correspondent he had seen and talked to soldiers near death. He recognized the signs.

"Last will and testament," Al said, motioning weakly toward a paper sticking out of his Bible. "It's all for you ... know you'll do the right thing ... all for you, Ed, 'cause you know the truth."

Alan Sutton's ragged breathing grew more and more irregular as he slipped into unconsciousness. Ed Weeks watched his friend's life ebb away as the impact of Al's final request hit him.

So, the world awaited a solution to a mystery disappearance almost as big as that of Jimmy Hoffa. And Ed Weeks had uncovered the answer. But Ed Weeks had also inherited $50 million. How could he write objectively now? Who would believe him? "All for you ... do the right thing ... 'cause you know the truth," the ragged whisper echoed as Alan Sutton died. Visions of Lear jets, yachts, penthouse apartments and Riviera casinos flashed through Ed's mind. What *was* the truth? It had all seemed so simple before. Ed Weeks couldn't believe his bad luck.

Epiphany 4
Mark 1:21-28

Casting Out Demons

Just then there was in their synagogue a man with an unclean spirit, and he cried out, "What have you to do with us, Jesus of Nazareth? Have you come to destroy us? I know who you are, the Holy One of God." But Jesus rebuked him, saying, "Be silent, and come out of him!" And the unclean spirit, convulsing him and crying with a loud voice, came out of him.

— verses 23-26

There was once a deeply troubled church that could not keep any pastor for more than a year or two. Eight pastors had come and gone in eleven years, all of them at the request of the congregation after controversy with one of the long-time leaders. The church blamed the Bishop for sending them inept pastors. The pastors blamed the congregation, saying that ministry was impossible with a people so intent on self-destruction. Many members left, and, in time, no pastor could be found who was willing to serve what everyone was calling "that difficult charge."

Finally, in exasperation, the Bishop called a special meeting which included several key leaders from the troubled congregation and forty lay and clergy members of her Annual Conference, chosen randomly. She invited the leaders of the congregation to describe the difficulties they had experienced over the past several years. Then the District Superintendent was given an opportunity to tell the story from his point of view. Many questions were asked of the superintendent and the congregational leaders. When everyone had had a say, the Bishop addressed the whole gathering in her best preacher's voice, saying, "Brothers and sisters, what are we going to do? Whom shall we send to this tormented congregation to share with them the healing power of Jesus the Christ?"

Then the Bishop invited everyone to pray silently with her. The silence lasted for a long time and continued even after the Bishop concluded the prayer with a resolute "amen." At last one of the older pastors spoke out from the back of the room. "I'll go," she said. There was a collective gasp, and then a sustained buzzing of voices that started out low and grew until it filled the room. Everyone knew that she had been on leave of absence for several years and that she had left her last church in the wake of a scandalous divorce. She had become an alcoholic, been twice convicted of drunk driving, had spent six months in prison and a month in a chemical dependency treatment center. There had been some talk of removing her orders, but since she was so near retirement she had been allowed to keep her credentials in consideration of her many years of faithful service and the progress she had made in her rehabilitation program. The Bishop and the superintendents had hoped to place her with some small, quiet, caring congregation where she could serve her remaining years without stress.

"Are you sure, Deborah?" the Bishop asked. "This is a very difficult assignment."

"This is a congregation in pain," Deborah said. "I know something about pain. I think I should be the one to go." Heads could be seen nodding all around the room. Everyone knew in that moment that the Spirit had moved among them. "There is one condition to my going, however," Deborah said to the Bishop. "You must give me a free hand to do whatever is necessary to bring about healing. I must know that I have your full support to do what is needed." The Bishop looked back at Deborah, and, without blinking an eye, said, "You have my full support to do whatever is needed."

Deborah and the District Superintendent met with the leaders of the troubled congregation after the meeting. They agreed to accept her as their pastor, although they expressed some surprise that a woman her age would want to take on such a difficult task. Near the end of the meeting, Deborah asked for the same unconditional support she had requested of the Bishop. They agreed to give her free reign to do whatever was needed to help heal the congregation, and, at Deborah's insistence, they solemnly promised to pray for her every day. Then she told them what she planned to do to begin the healing process. She said, "It is my intention to visit with every member of this congregation before I perform any other pastoral duties, including preaching. I will not lead worship or attend any meetings until that task is finished. I suggest that you arrange for someone else to lead the worship services over the next few weeks. I'll let you know when I am ready to preach." The chair of the committee looked at the superintendent. The superintendent nodded and the chairperson said, "I'll make the arrangements."

Deborah began her visitation the following day. She went from house to house, apartment to apartment, hospital bed to nursing home bed, introducing herself as the new pastor and asking each one, as she went, to respond to two questions: How did you come to love Jesus, and why have you chosen to serve him in this congregation? She visited morning, afternoon and evening for four-and-a-half weeks and was warmly received by every member of the congregation but one. Then she went home, called the lay leader, and told him she would be prepared to preach the following Sunday.

The sanctuary was packed that day. Almost every able member was present. They waited eagerly for the sermon to hear what Deborah would have to say. Her text was Mark 1:16-20, the calling of the disciples. She said, "I want to share two things with you today: How I came to love Jesus, and why I believe God has called me to serve him with you in this congregation." It was a stirring sermon. Many in the congregation were moved to tears. Then, just as Deborah was about to ask them to join with her in prayer, a man stood up in the back of the sanctuary and shouted out at her. It was Harry Wiersem, the man who had refused to see her when she called at his home. He was the long-time leader who had bedeviled so many pastors before her. Some had told Deborah that he had never recovered from the death of his wife many years before.

"Who do you think you are, sister?" he yelled. "We know all about you. You couldn't keep your husband and you are a drunk. You're the last thing we need in this church. We've got enough problems as it is!"

He stood glaring at her, his face red and his knuckles bulging white as his hands gripped the pew in front of him. Deborah looked back at him with sad eyes. She didn't speak for several seconds. It seemed like an eternity to the congregation. It was absolutely silent in the sanctuary. No one moved or seemed to breathe.

"I am a sinner, Harry," Deborah said in a soft, firm voice, still looking into his angry, red face. "A forgiven sinner. And I've come to serve with sinners: forgiven sinners." Then she stepped down from the pulpit and walked up the long center aisle to where Harry was still hanging on to the back of his pew. She put her arm around his shoulder, looked him in the eye and said, "I am sorry about Mildred. She must have been very dear to you." Harry let go of the pew, fell into her arms and began to sob like a baby. When he was finished, Deborah bid everyone to gather round. They joined hands and she led them in prayer. When she said "Amen," Deborah was aware of something around her that felt like a collective sigh of relief. The demons were gone. The congregation would be whole again.

Deborah served with them for twelve years, retiring at last at the age of 74. Harry Wiersem became her most outspoken supporter, and, just before he died, told her that she had been an answer to prayer.

Author's note:
This story appeared in the May 1994 issue of *Circuit Rider* magazine under the title "Healing Words."

52

Epiphany 5
1 Corinthians 9:16-23

A Seat On Bill

I have become all things to all people, that I might by all means save some. I do it all for the sake of the Gospel, so that I may share in its blessings.

— verses 22b-23

My friend Bill Benson was a successful small town businessman. His little grocery store stayed open long after many of the other businesses in Willow Bluff had succumbed to the overwhelming competition of the big chain warehouse stores that have moved into the city over the past ten years. People were glad to be able to buy their groceries locally and often thanked Bill for making it possible. But this is not what Bill will be remembered for. Bill will be remembered for the bench he often occupied in front of the store, and for the transforming difference his presence there made in a great many lives.

Hardly an afternoon passed in good weather when Bill was not seen holding court on the long park bench which sat to the right of the store's main entrance, under the awning that shaded the large picture window. Everyone stopped to talk to Bill. Hank, the barber, would come over to sip pop on his afternoon break. Gloria, from the beauty shop, and some of the bank tellers would stop by during their breaks. Cattle truckers on their way back from the auction barn would pull in to get a candy bar and visit with Bill. Bert, the newspaper editor; Shirley, from the insurance office; Gil and Herb, from the feedmill; Ralph, the funeral director; and Evelyn, our town lawyer, all found their way sooner or later to Bill's bench. On slow afternoons in the real estate office, my secretary always knew to look for me over at Bill's.

My most cherished memories are of the times we sat there alone, before others came or after they had gone back to work. Bill was a good listener. I could tell him my troubles and know not only that he understood, but also that he would not betray my confidence. It was during one of these conversations, many years ago, that Bill offered to pray for me. Things were rocky in my marriage. I was beside myself. I was afraid Jenny was going to take the kids and leave me. Bill's prayer helped me put things into perspective. I began to pray regularly myself. Jenny and I went to a counselor and gradually we worked out our differences.

It was shortly after this that Bill invited me to go to church with him on Sunday. He was so gentle, so winsome in the way he asked, that I could think of no kind way to refuse. I owed him too much. So I went to church with Bill that Sunday, thinking once would be enough to repay my debt. I have been going back every Sunday now for thirty years.

Oh, how we miss Bill in the church. Half of us are there because of him and his bench-warming. I was one of many who went to church and came to love Jesus because of Bill's loving presence on that bench. The man had an irresistible passion for sharing his faith.

I visit Bill's grave almost every evening when I go for my walk down by the river. I always end up at the cemetery. I laughed out loud the first time I saw his tombstone and read the inscription. The stone is shaped in the form of a simple bench. The epitaph, chiseled in bold letters below the seat, reads, "HAVE A SEAT ON BILL."

Epiphany 6
2 Kings 5:1-14

One In Need Of Healing: Naaman's Story

*Elisha sent a messenger to him, saying, "Go, wash in the
Jordan seven times, and your flesh shall be restored and
you shall be clean."*

— verse 10

You may recall that when Jesus preached on this text in his
home synagogue, they chased him out of town and tried to throw
him over a cliff. And all he said was:

*"There were also many lepers in Israel in the time of the
prophet Elisha, and none of them was cleansed except
Naaman, the Syrian."*

— Luke 4:27

But that was enough.

*When they heard this, all in the synagogue were filled
with rage.*

— Luke 4:28

We would all be well advised to be careful where and how we
tell this story.

I stand before you today as one in need of healing, as Naaman
was, as we all are.

We come here in our brokenness, suffering as we all do from
the diseases of racism, sexism, nationalism, denominationalism and
homophobia. Some of us come bearing the scars of dysfunctional
families: sexual, physical and emotional abuse — both abusers and
abused — some of us hurting from wounds we have received from
brothers and sisters sitting in these same pews.

55

We come with all of our pathologies: physical, emotional and spiritual, with all of our fears and griefs, into this community of recovering, forgiven sinners, this sinful and holy, dysfunctional and redeeming church — seeking healing.

And I, for one, am glad to be here in this community where I have been both abused and loved, where I have both sinned and been forgiven. And where I have been healed.

I cannot come into this place without thinking of my uncle, Donald Sumwalt, who, as some of you remember, was the registrar of this event for many years. He and I always sat together at the communion service on the last day. I will be thinking of him on Thursday as we come together in that service — and will remember, as I always do, what he did for me on my first ordination day in June of 1976. We were all together at the American Baptist Assembly in Green Lake. My wife Jo and I were tenting in the campground there. Uncle Don and Aunt Hazel were in a camper in a lot next to ours. I woke up on ordination Sunday with a knot in my back about the size of a grapefruit. It was all I could do to lift myself out of the sleeping bag. Every movement caused excruciating pain. I didn't know how I was going to get dressed, let alone walk up an aisle, kneel down and be ordained. Uncle Don came over and told me to lie down on my stomach. Then he laid hands on me and massaged my back muscles until I was able to walk. When Bishop Jesse DeWitt laid his hands on me later that morning, I knew I was being ordained into a healing community.

It was two years after that, in 1978, that Uncle Don was diagnosed with multiple myeloma, a cancer of the bone. The doctors did not expect him to live more than three months. He would not accept their prognosis. He prayed and we all prayed, and he felt assurance that he would be healed for ministry. He was. He served eight more years at Juda and at Chippewa Falls before his death in 1986. This is a community in which people are healed.

I gave thanks as I opened my travel kit this morning that two items were not there that I have had to bring with me in some years past — my Maalox bottle and my valium prescription. During the book controversy in Montello in 1981, and again during the building project in 1984, I suffered a stress-related stomach disorder. Lloyd

Rediger helped me to give up some of my co-dependent and workaholic behavior — to "try smarter not harder" as he used to preach to all of us. I have learned to manage my stress by jogging and by taking regular days off. I am learning that I am not responsible for everything my church does or doesn't do — and to resist my obsession to try to control everything. I grow tomatoes now and I play softball (which is a different kind of disease). I understand myself to be in recovery. I experience healing and I give thanks for healing almost every day.

During those two dark years when I was sick, much sicker than I realized at the time (when I came here to this place, to this school for ministry, wondering if I would ever be completely well again and fearing that I would have to give up the work I loved), there were persons here who listened to me as I expressed my hurt and literally put their arms around me and loved me enough that I was able to go home and continue my work with hope. This is a healing community!

Those of us who are clergy tell our families and our congregations, as they watch us pack our golf clubs and our tennis rackets, that we come here for academic lectures and workshops (we are required to do it, you know — continuing education). But they know, and we know too, if we are honest with ourselves, that we really come here to be healed. There are other places we could go for lectures and workshops.

We come here to soak our weary souls in long, warm conversations with friends: to be immersed again in the restorative fellowship of kindred spirits and anointed with the healing oil of laughter. We come to break bread together, here in front of the altar, in the fellowship hall across the way, and in the cafes, restaurants and pizza joints downtown. Damrows over here on College Avenue serves the best oatmeal and the best toasted whole grain bread in the world. It is a holy place where one can savor an early morning cup of coffee and enjoy the companionship of good friends. Rabbi Jesus sometimes comes in and opens our eyes for us. And there is a bar over here on the northwest side which serves the hottest chili this side of Texas. All of this, our lectures and workshops, the exchange of new ideas, the sharing of hurts and joys, the prayers we pray, the songs we sing, pick-up basketball games, shopping sprees, late night outings to the movies, solitary walks, quiet discussions with superintendents: all of this is healing.

The young, captive girl who served in Naaman's household, were she alive today, could confidently send the Naamans of our time to this body of Christ. This is a healing community! And it will remain, long after this school for ministry is over, a community in need of healing. For we healers are also sinners, and we are continually wounding each other and being wounded by the sin-corrupted systems which plague our institutional life.

There is one corrupt system in particular which causes us more pain than anything else in our beloved church, and if it is not healed it will certainly be the death of United Methodism. That is the appointment system, our peculiar method of marrying pastors and congregations. It is more than a little ironic that we United Methodists, who are so much committed to egalitarian principles in government, in the market place, in education and the arts, and to democratic reform around the world, should cling so assiduously to such an autocratic method of choosing servant leaders. I think our late brother, John Wesley, who had no wish to leave the Church of England or to break its rules, who was repulsed by the thought of preaching in the fields and streets, who was most reluctant to allow lay persons to preach and to ordain lay preachers on his own authority, who resisted to his dying day the formation of a separate church — I think John Wesley would understand our reluctance to break with familiar traditions. But as he could not deny the spirit — the holy, healing spirit — neither can we.

We cannot be whole and healthy and joy-filled in this United Methodist movement until lay persons and pastors in our local churches share appointment power equally, and in a fully collegial way, with district superintendents and bishops. No, I am not suggesting that we adopt a call system. Connectionalism is our strength. Let bishops and district superintendents continue to be strong advocates for shared mission. The world is indeed our parish, now even more than it was for John Wesley. But we will not be able to minister effectively in the world of the twenty-first century if we perpetuate the eighteenth century hierarchical power structures that cause so much suffering among pastors and local congregations who are left out of the power loop.

How can we be healed?

Perhaps in the same way that Namaan was healed.

Naaman's Story

Naaman was a man like Norman Schwarzkopf of our own time, a hero of the nation, a commander of the army, held in high regard by the commander-in-chief because of his victories in battle. Imagine the reaction of the American public if it became known that such a man, though a mighty warrior, had AIDS. And can you imagine what the reaction would be if the President of the United States sent our Naaman off to visit the President of Cuba, let's say, carrying a letter like the one the King of Aram sent to the King of Israel. Do you think Mr. Castro might have reason to wonder about our President's intentions?

The general would arrive in Havana on Air Force One, carrying a trunkload of American dollars, a couple of Cadillacs and several tickets to next year's Super Bowl game. A limousine would whisk him off to the prophet's house, where he would be met by a secretary wearing latex gloves and bearing a message from the prophet telling him to go wash in the Bay of Pigs. We can understand why a general of the United States Army might be infuriated by such a suggestion. The Persian Gulf or the Panama Canal maybe, but not the Bay of Pigs!

Naaman would have been well aware that it was just east of the Jordan, in the time of the Israelite King Ahab, that his nation had suffered one of its most ignominious defeats. One hundred thousand Aramaean soldiers were slaughtered by the Israelites and the Aramaean king was captured. Wash in the Jordan indeed! But somehow his advisors were able to convince him to do it. And he was healed, as he had hoped, but not in the way he expected.

Naaman, whose power in Aram was second only to that of the king, could find no healing there. The Spirit, through the most unlikely voice of a young slave girl, sent him to another nation, to the prophet of a God he did not know.

Through whom will the spirit speak to us? In what dirty little river will God have us wash our leprous church?

Majid Tehranian, director of the Peace Institute in Honolulu, said in a speech recently:

> *All of us live with three kinds of lies: the lies we tell others, the lies we tell ourselves, and the lies we don't even know we are telling, or, more accurately, living.*

Tehranian said,

> *We know the lies we tell to others; the lies we tell ourselves are a bit harder to discern, but the only way to really grasp the lies we don't even know we are living is to get outside our own cultural setting.*
>
> (*The Christian Century*, p. 635, July 1, 1992)

In this case it might help at least to get outside our own denomination.

There is a prophet in the Roman Catholic Church by the name of William Rademacher who has written about these issues in a book called *Lay Ministry* (Cross Roads Publishing Co., 1991).

Rademacher describes several institutional pathologies which plague his beloved Roman church:

> *Patriarchy, fear of women in ministry, obsession with secrecy, the preoccupation with sex, the compulsive need to control (especially the selection of bishops), and the fear of sharing real authority ...*

"... a pathology," he says, "that is evident in the tight control and secrecy in the hierarchic system that selects only ultrasafe men as bishops." "Prophets," he adds, "are avoided like the plague" (p. 105).

Rademacher gives this qualified hope:

> *Since these pathologies have become part of its identity, the church is afraid to let them go ... Giving them up will*

60

require a wrenching emotional death ... True reform will require a miracle of grace, an intervention by the spirit, "like the rush of a mighty wind" coming from outside the church. (p. 106)

One of our own prophets, Don Ott, said upon his election as Bishop recently:

We are seen by many within the church and outside as an institution that has lost its way in our world. We need to throw the windows open and say to ourselves we must think in new ways and must be adaptable as we can in the rules established to govern our lives.

(The Milwaukee Sentinel, July, 1992)

"... throw open the windows ... and think in new ways ..."

Our United Methodist Church will be healed when we are able to heed that call. When, like Naaman, we are willing to go where the Spirit leads and do what the Spirit bids, our spirits will be restored like the spirit of a young child and we will be clean. We will be clean!

Author's Note:

John preached this sermon at a healing service at The Wisconsin Conference of The United Methodist Church's School For Ministry at First United Methodist Church in Appleton, Wisconsin, August 18, 1992.

The Aqueduct

I am about to do a new thing; now it springs forth, do you not perceive it? I will make a way in the wilderness and rivers in the desert. The wild animals will honor me, the jackals and the ostriches; for I give water in the wilderness, rivers in the desert, to give drink to my chosen people, the people whom I formed for myself so that they might declare my praise.

But you have burdened me with your sins; you have wearied me with your iniquities.

— verses 19-21, 24b

Years ago there was an aqueduct that brought fresh water into the center of the village, all the way from the lake near the top of the mountain. It had been carefully constructed so that gravity carried the water even over steep inclines and around sharp bends. The man who built the aqueduct was very wise and had devoted his entire life to its completion. Now all that remained of the ancient waterway were a few weathered pillars here and there along the path.

Women told this story to their children as they followed the path up the mountain to fetch water from the lake. Some of the women said that they could remember their grandmothers telling of a time when water flowed directly into the village. But for as long as any of them could remember, women had climbed the mountain daily to get fresh water for their families. "What happened to the aqueduct?" the children would always ask. And the answer was always the same. "It was destroyed many years ago in a war with another village."

The story was told for generations, as women trudged up and down the mountain carrying the heavy jars of water on their heads and in their hands, until at last a young woman named Esther declared that she would rebuild the aqueduct. Everyone laughed at her. "It can't be done," they said. "The engineering knowledge that it would take to build such a thing has long been lost. There is no one among us who is wise enough to build an aqueduct — and certainly it could not be built by a woman." But Esther did not give up. She was determined to see the aqueduct rebuilt in her lifetime. While other young women were marrying and raising their children, Esther studied and planned. She read books on building and she journied to the far side of the mountain to talk to builders from other villages. One day she met an old man who had once helped in the construction of an aqueduct. Esther asked him many questions and the man told her as much as he knew. When he was finished, Esther returned to her village certain that she now had enough knowledge to build the aqueduct. She drew up a plan and began recruiting men and women to help with the building. The men refused to help at first, but they soon saw that it was a workable plan, and then they joined gladly in the labor. In just fifteen years the aqueduct was completed and fresh water again flowed into the center of the village.

The aqueduct served the village for many years, until the time came when no one remembered when water had been carried by head and hand. It never occurred to them, when war broke out with a village on the other side of the mountain, that the aqueduct might be destroyed, or what it would mean to live without it. If they had known, they might have guarded the aqueduct more carefully, or perhaps they would have chosen not to go to war at all. This became part of the story that the women told their children, after the war was over, as they trudged up the mountain every day to fetch fresh water for their families. "What happened to the aqueduct?" the children asked. And the answer was always the same.

Dor's Vision

Six days later, Jesus took with him Peter and James and John, and led them up a high mountain apart, by themselves. And he was transfigured before them, and his clothes became dazzling white, such as no one on earth could bleach them.

— verses 2-3

As I lay in St. Luke's Hospital, being prepared for an aortagram, I felt quite apprehensive. An aortagram is similar to an angiogram, but instead of sending a little liquid through an artery, lots of *warm, warm* liquid courses through the aorta while doctors monitor the heart's action by x-ray.

In the midst of my anxiety, I reminded myself that many, many friends were surrounding me with prayers. Then I realized that it was time for *me* to ask for help. I prayed to God in the best way I knew how.

Almost immediately I felt myself gently floating up the path of the whitest, brightest light I had ever seen. I was floating toward a bright, bright opening, when suddenly a large, radiant, white figure picked me up and held me. What I had prayed was to be lifted by his right hand, and this seemed to be it! Such a wonderful, peaceful feeling!

Now and then I heard the voice of the x-ray technician asking, "Are you all right, Mrs. Miller?" Soon he said, "We're nearly finished."

Knowing that God had really answered my prayer, I turned around to give him my thanks, BUT I COULD NOT SEE HIS FACE: only the radiant light ... and Jesus was in front of him, holding me up.

A moment later, my mom and dad came near me and said, "Dor, you're going to be all right." They smiled, and then just faded away. The brilliant opening closed and the light disappeared.

The radiologist said, "We're finished, and we'll soon have you back in your own room." I had made it through the test, which I was *later* told can sometimes result in the patient suffering a stroke during the process!

I now feel that I know the meaning of grace and being born again. Love and faith are the answers.

Author's note:
Thank you to Dorothy Miller for this account of her experience.

Ash Wednesday
Psalm 51:1-18

Old Granddad

Create in me a clean heart, O God, and put a new and right spirit within me. Do not cast me away from your presence, and do not take your holy spirit from me. Restore to me the joy of your salvation, and sustain in me a willing spirit. Then I will teach transgressors your ways, and sinners will return to you.

— verses 10-13

Charlie Johnson was up at 5:30, had all of his gear in the trunk of the car, and was drinking coffee when Martha came downstairs.

"Are you going fishing again?" was her good morning greeting.

"Don't know whether to go or not," grumbled Charlie, "but I guess I will. Old Granddad's a-waitin'."

Martha didn't need an explanation for that comment. A week ago Charlie had been at "the hole" (that's how he referred to that spot on the river where he'd fished for nearly 50 years) and had had a very unpleasant encounter with "a bunch of young punks" as he called them. He had been in search, as always, of "Old Granddad." That's how all the area anglers referred to the biggest, meanest, most elusive old catfish on the river. People had been seeing that lunker for 15 years, but nobody had been able to set a hook in him ... yet. Charlie was sure it was just a matter of time and few, if any, spent more time trying. Well, that day a week ago, when Charlie got to the hole, he had company waiting. Four "young punks" were already there, and just a few yards from Charlie's spot. He tried to fish, but he couldn't get much done that day because of the noise.

"Why, those kids didn't sit still for five minutes," he later told Martha. "They were whoopin' and hollerin' and carryin' on ... runnin' around. Why, they made enough noise to wake the dead. There's no WAY there'd be any fish around!"

66

Certainly not Old Granddad.

"I'm tellin' you, Martha, these young people today ain't worth their salt, the whole lot of 'em. They don't have any values, and they don't show no respect for nobody. The whole generation ain't worth a plug nickel. The world's in a sad state of affairs if THEY are our future!"

Well, that was how Charlie felt, and it had taken more than a week to get him back in the mood to wet a line again. Martha was glad he was going, but she hoped there wouldn't be any more unpleasantness. He'd probably be back by noon. Maybe she'd fix something special for lunch, just in case. Pork chops with gravy and mashed potatoes was Charlie's favorite. Maybe some fresh baked cherry pie for dessert.

Charlie arrived at "the hole" right on the dot at 6:15. And he was alone this time. By 6:30 he had a couple of nice largemouth on the stringer, but no sign yet of Old Granddad. Then some twigs snapped, and Charlie wasn't alone anymore.

A boy of about sixteen came through the bushes next to the railroad track and set up to fish about twenty yards downstream from Charlie. "Name's Joey," he called. "Catchin' any?"

"Charlie. Nothin' much," was the reluctant reply.

Nothing else was said for a long time. Joey pulled in a couple of bass of his own. Charlie hooked another and threw back two bullheads and a red horse. About 8:00, Charlie pulled his line in to bait up. For some reason, he glanced back toward the river and there was that shadow he'd seen so many times! Old Granddad was on the prowl. But Charlie's hook was in his hand, NOT in the water. He began to hurry, but that was always when Charlie became "all thumbs": couldn't find the worms, couldn't get the worm on, then couldn't pick up the pole. Finally he got it all together and cast back into "the hole."

About the time he sat back down he heard a kind of gasp and looked toward Joey, whose expression was one of complete wonder, and whose pole was bent nearly double.

Charlie looked in total disbelief as young Joey ... just a KID, mind you ... did what he hadn't been able to do for nearly fifteen years. Joey hooked, battled and beached Old Granddad! Not without some coaching and cheering from Charlie, however, who made it over to Joey's spot in about two seconds flat. He just couldn't help but get excited because he'd only ever had a hook in Old Granddad once in all that time, and the wily cat had slipped off. Other than that, Charlie didn't even know anyone who'd come close to catching Old Granddad. Now here was this punk kid holding him up by the gills. It was unbelievable.

"Quick, mister … er … Charlie. Could you get the camera out of my backpack?"

So, Charlie — unwilling witness that he was — snapped the picture of Joey and Old Granddad. Charlie put the camera back in the kid's bag and turned around to the riverbank just in time to see Old Granddad splash and swim away.

"What are you doing?" roared Charlie. "I've been trying to get him for 15 years, and you let him go?"

"Well," Joey said calmly, "that was the one they call Old Granddad, wasn't it? People been trying to catch him since I was in diapers. Maybe longer. Today he made one mistake and got hooked. Doesn't seem right to condemn him to the dinner table for one little mistake."

Charlie scraped the plate with his fork for the last little bits of pie crust and filling. "Martha," he said, "there was someone else at the fishing hole today. The Smith boy from over on Daley Lane."

"Oh, yes. Joey," said Martha. "Hope he didn't give you any trouble."

"You know, Martha, maybe ALL kids today aren't like the ones I saw last week … I think maybe Joey and I will go out again in the morning."

Author's Note:
This story was written and told by my brother, Rod Perry, at a benefit storytelling concert John and I did for Passages, a women's shelter in Richland Center, Wisconsin. When I was growing up, my "big brother" was one of the joys of my life. It was his finely-honed sense of the ridiculous that helped to shape mine, and his

instruction in the fine arts — the humor of Homer and Jethro, Stan Freberg, Spike Jones, Bob Newhart, Jonathan Winters and Charlie Weaver — that prepared me for life out in the world. Our thanks to him for allowing us to print this story. I love you, Roddy!

Lent 1
Psalm 25:1-10

Fearless Freddie

---

*Do not remember the sins of my youth or my trans-
gressions; according to your steadfast love remember me,
for your goodness' sake, O Lord! Good and upright is
the Lord; therefore he instructs sinners in the way. He
leads the humble in what is right, and teaches the humble
his way.*

— verses 7-9

Once upon a time there was a boy known as Fearless Freddie.
They called him Fearless because he wasn't afraid of anything. He
wasn't afraid of the dark. He wasn't afraid of rats or snakes. He
wasn't afraid of climbing tall trees. Freddie wasn't even afraid of
the big, mean dog in Mrs. Polkinghorn's back yard! Freddie's
mother used to say, "Freddie, you be careful! You might get hurt!"
But Freddie would say, "Aw, Mom, I won't get hurt. I'm not afraid
of anything."

Then one day, while Freddie and some of his friends were
walking along the rock quarry a few blocks from the park, a strong
wind blew up suddenly and carried his hat over the edge of the
quarry. It landed on a narrow ledge about three feet down from the
top. "Wait a minute, guys," Freddie said. "I have to go get my
hat."

"Aren't you afraid of going down there?" one of his friends
asked. "It's a long way to the bottom of the quarry. If you slip,
you'll get killed."

"Aw, don't worry," Freddie said. "I'm not afraid of anything."

Freddie climbed over the edge of the quarry, and, without being
the least bit careful, lowered himself down to the narrow ledge. He
walked several feet along the ledge, and just as he was within reach
of the hat, one of his feet slipped and he slid over the edge toward
the bottom of the quarry, about sixty feet below. Luckily for Freddie,

his jacket sleeve caught on the branch of a bush that was growing in a crevice below the ledge, and he was left dangling, almost in mid-air, held fast by the bush.

"Help! Help!" Freddie cried out. "I'm going to fall. Somebody help me!"

One of Freddie's friends ran to get help. Soon the rescue squad arrived with ropes and ladders. One of the men climbed over the edge of the quarry and tied a rope around Freddie's waist. Then he and the rest of the rescue team hoisted Freddie up to the top. They also retrieved his hat.

As soon as his feet were safely on the ground, Freddie said, "I was very, very scared. Thank you for saving my life."

They never, ever called him Fearless Freddie again.

Afflicted

For he did not despise or abhor the affliction of the afflicted; he did not hide his face from me, but heard when I cried to him.

— verse 24

There was once a little boy whose most prized possession was a light blue cat's-eye crystal marble. "Big Blue," as he called it, sparkled in the sunlight like a raindrop and glistened in the moonlight like a diamond. The little boy always carried it in his pocket so he could rub it for good luck. Sometimes he would take Big Blue out and show it to his friends, but most often he played with it by himself on lazy summer afternoons as he hiked along the beach when there was nothing else to do.

One Saturday morning, the little boy was playing with Big Blue on the beach. He rolled the marble down toward the breaking waves to see how close he could come without getting it wet. Suddenly one of the biggest boys in the neighborhood appeared, as if out of nowhere, grabbed up the marble and ran off with it as fast as he could. The little boy chased after him but the big boy was much too fast for him.

The little boy was so shaken he didn't know what to do. His parents had warned him about playing alone on the beach. What would they say now, when they found out he had disobeyed them? He couldn't bring himself to tell them, and he didn't know of anyone else he could trust.

Months passed and the little boy still had not told a soul about what had happened to him on the beach. Then he had an idea. The little boy knew exactly what he had to do.

He went to the big boy's house, ran up the front steps, marched across the porch and rang the doorbell. The big boy's mama opened the door. "What do you want?" she asked in a harsh voice.

"I want my big blue marble back," the little boy said. "Your son took it from me and I want it back!"

"I don't know what you're talking about," the big boy's mama said. "My boy would never do anything like that! You get away from here and don't come back." With that, she slammed the door with a big bang.

The little boy sat down on the last step and thought about what he should do next. After a while, something inside him seemed to say, "Go ask her again. Keep asking until you get what belongs to you." So the little boy got up and knocked on the door again. When the big boy's mama saw him, she closed the curtains and shouted for him to go away.

The little boy did go away, but in a half-hour he was back again, carrying a white sign nailed to a narrow board. On the sign, in large blue letters, he had printed, "GIVE ME BACK MY MARBLE!" The little boy began to march up and down in front of the big boy's house, holding the sign up high and shouting at the top of his voice, "Give me back my marble! Give me back my marble!"

Soon there was a large crowd gathered in front of the big boy's house. A van from the television station rolled up and some people got out and began to film the little boy's small demonstration. A woman with a microphone interviewed the little boy. He told how the big boy had taken his marble and that he had come to his house to get it back.

About an hour after the interview had been broadcast on the nightly news, several other little boys arrived. They said the big boy had stolen their marbles, too. Then, one by one, they all fell in line behind the little boy as he marched back and forth in front of the big boy's house. They held up signs, too, and they joined the little boy, shouting at the tops of their voices: "Give us back our marbles! Give us back our marbles!"

Suddenly the door opened and the big boy's mama appeared on the porch with a bag of candy. "Come, sit down," she said, "have some candy. We can work this thing out without so much fuss." The little boys stopped shouting and they put down their signs, but they didn't take any of the candy.

The big boy's mama said, "Let's be reasonable about this. Here's a dollar for each of you. Now, go to the store and buy yourselves some more marbles and don't bother us anymore."

Not one of the little boys spoke a word. They simply turned their backs on the big boy's mama, lifted up their signs and began to march all the way around the house, shouting at the tops of their voices, "Give us back our marbles! Give us back our marbles!" They marched and shouted and shouted and marched and marched and shouted until it was dark. Then they all went home and went to bed. The next morning, right after breakfast, they were all back again marching and shouting at the tops of their voices, "Give us back our marbles! Give us back our marbles."

This went on for several days until at last the door opened again and the big boy's mama came out and said in a nasty voice, "Here, take your stinking marbles." Then she spat on each one and rolled them all into the ash pile on the end of the porch. The little boys ceased their shouting, put down their signs and walked slowly and sadly over to the ash heap to retrieve their soiled marbles.

The little boy was the last to find his beloved Big Blue. It was so dirty he could hardly see any blue at all and the sparkle was nowhere to be seen. The little boy walked down to the beach and dipped Big Blue into the waves. Then he wiped it on his shirt and held it up to be warmed by the sun. The little boy's face lit up into a great smile as he saw Big Blue catch the rays of the sun and begin to sparkle like a raindrop. "I got Big Blue back, I got Big Blue back!" he shouted over and over again as he held the marble up in the sun and ran along the beach as fast as his legs could run.

74

You Shall Not Murder

There was once a man who was an active proponent of capital punishment. He wrote hundreds of letters to the editor, circulated petitions door to door, testified in public hearings, and lobbied his state legislators and congresspersons to enact strict laws requiring the death penalty for every kind of murder. "A life for a life," he was fond of saying. "That's what it says in the scriptures."

One day, after a party celebrating the enactment of one of the laws he had long sought, this same man drove his car the wrong way up a one-way street and crashed into a minivan carrying a mother and her two small children. The mother and one of the children died instantly. The other child died later in the hospital. A Breathalyzer test proved the man guilty of drunk driving. He was convicted of manslaughter and sentenced to three years in prison. His lawyer assured him he would be out in a matter of months and would soon be driving again. As the sheriff's officer led the man out of the courtroom in handcuffs to begin serving his sentence, he was met on the courthouse steps by a group of demonstrators carrying signs which read, "Death to Drunk Drivers!" "Death to All Murderers!"

In that same community there was another man who was a strong advocate for the repeal of all death penalty laws. He wrote hundreds of letters to the editor, circulated petitions door to door, testified in public hearings and led candlelight vigils outside the state prison on the nights before scheduled executions. "Blessed are the merciful," he was fond of saying, "for they will receive mercy."

One day, this man received word that his only daughter and his two grandchildren had been killed by a drunk driver in an automobile crash. He was calm at first, but as the days passed his grief turned to anger, and then to rage. It was all he could do to contain himself as he sat in the courtroom on the day that the killer was sentenced to only three years in prison. He knew this man who had so carelessly taken his daughter's life would be released in a matter of months. He watched helplessly as the police officer led the prisoner out of the courtroom and down the courthouse steps. He listened as the crowd began to chant, "Death to drunk drivers!" "Death to all murderers!" Then slowly, deliberately, as if in a dream, he pulled a gun from his pocket and began to fire at the man who had taken the light out of his life.

Dog Days Of The Soul

"And this is the judgment, that the light has come into the world, and people loved darkness rather than light because their deeds were evil. For all who do evil hate the light and do not come to the light, so that their deeds may not be exposed. But those who do what is true come to the light, so that it may be clearly seen that their deeds have been done in God."

— verses 19-21

Introduction

Have you ever been sitting in a lighted room at night, reading or talking, and suddenly have the lights go out? What's the first thing you say? Sometimes everyone says it together: "Who turned out the light?"

In this age of electricity, light is something we take for granted. Few of us ever experience total darkness. In the city, we have street lights which come on automatically as soon as it begins to get dark. In the country, most farms have a mercury vapor light that stays on all night for security reasons. Consequently, most of us never get a good look at the stars as we used to when all the lights went out at night.

Some of the soldiers who came back from the Persian Gulf War told about the absolute darkness they experienced in the desert. One soldier said, "The darkness on nights with no moon or star light was so total you could have been standing right next to someone and not known it."

This text from John's gospel is about darkness and light: "And this is the judgment," John says, "that the light has come into the world and people loved darkness rather than light because their deeds were evil."

Is it possible John is right, that we really love darkness rather than light?

We always light candles at the conclusion of our Chrismas Eve services. We turn out all of the lights in the church sanctuary and we hold our candle flames up in the darkness as we sing "Silent Night." It is a mystical moment in which one's soul is warmed by a wondrous, transcendent grace. The light Christ brings into the world seems almost tangible. We can see it and feel it and the truth to which the symbol points comes alive in our hearts. But then we go home and turn on the evening news and hear about drug deals, drive-by shootings, homelessness, unemployment, racism, ethnic cleansing, genocide, child abuse, rape, murder and terrorist bombings. The evils of the world seem to overwhelm the light.

There is also the darkness in our own souls, in our families, our churches, our schools and workplaces in the form of broken relationships, hate, suspicion, gossip, innuendo, heartache, depression and grief. Who turned out the light? John says we turn it out ourselves by our sin, by our evil deeds because we have "... loved darkness rather than light."

We cannot live without light. Light is something every living being has to have. Put a plant in a dark room and it will die or remain dormant until it is brought back into the light. We human beings can become depressed if we don't get enough sunlight. The technical name for this is Seasonal Affective Disorder or S.A.D. Syndrome, and the cure is simply more light, either artificial or natural. There is something about the light.

Those of us who live in the Midwest and suffer the long, cold winters of this region often experience what we call cabin fever or winter blahs. It comes from a lack of social interaction. The remedy is to get together with other people and have some fun. Worship is as good an excuse as any other, maybe better.

Dog Days

This has been an especially harsh winter compared to most: record snowfalls, record cold and windchill, record bouts with cold and flu viruses, pneumonia and other diseases of winter. We have had more people in the hospital in our community this winter than usual, and more deaths.

I call this time we have just passed through, the 46 days between Groundhog Day and the first day of Spring, the dog days of winter. The dog days of summer come during the hot and sultry month of August — you know, when it is so hot and humid you don't have energy to do anything. What we have just had are the dog days of winter, when it is so cloudy, and so damp and dreary and cold, that you don't care whether you do anything — and you begin to wonder if the winter blahs are going to last forever.

Our family has been going through some dog days recently. We have decided to get a d-d-d-d-dog-g-g-g. This is quite a turn-about for old Dad, who has always been the one in the family who has said, "No dogs!" Suffice it to say that I have been outvoted. Now, don't misunderstand me, I like dogs. I grew up with dogs on the farm, which is a good place to have dogs. I've just never been sure that I would like to live with a dog in the house. Cats are a different matter. Jo and I had cats in the early days of our married life and enjoyed them very much.

We got two cats from my folks, on the farm, about the time I started seminary. I thought they would be good company for Jo on the days, and some nights, while I was away at classes in Dubuque and she was home alone in the parsonage in Blue River.

That fall, when the weather turned cold, we started to notice mice around the house, and I began to grumble aloud in the presence of the cats, "What's the use of having cats if they don't keep mice out of the house?" One day, in utter frustration, I made a passing comment, again in the presence of both cats, that if they didn't start catching those mice I was going to start chopping their tails off an inch at a time.

The very next morning we were wakened by a commotion on the stairs that led up to our bedroom. Skitter, skitter, thump, thump. Skitter, skitter, thump, thump. Meow, Meow! It was our gray angora cat, Scratch, which was short for Beelzebub (we believed in giving our cats biblical names), and she had a big brown field mouse in her mouth. The poor mouse looked like the cat had been trying to lick him to death. He was sopping wet and very much alive. Scratch had clearly been playing with him for quite a while. She jumped up on to the bed with that mouse in her mouth and then let him go, as if to say it was our turn to play with him. The mouse ran across the bed covers and down onto the floor, and then climbed up the curtains on the window. Somehow we managed to catch both the mouse and the cat, and I took them down into the basement and carefully explained to them the facts of life about cats and mice.

Not more than two days later, our other cat, Maggie, which was short for Mary Magdelene (as I said, we believed in giving our cats religious names befitting their personalities), came into the family room carrying a live field mouse, and we went through the same thing all over again!

Anyway, we are going to get a dog. And the deal is that we are going to study all of the different breeds of dogs in the world and select one that best fits the needs of our family. The kids have been bringing home piles of dog books from the library, we've been talking to dog lovers, and Jo and I have been making secret visits to pet stores and kennels. We don't dare take the kids yet, because I know that the minute they see a cute puppy my dogless days are over. I figure this research and development phase ought to last two, maybe three years. But I may have miscalculated. Son Orrin has been making plans to con one of his grandfathers into building a doghouse. And last Saturday they all went out to a pet supply store and came home with a leash and a pooper scooper.

Ah, but the old man has one more ace in the hole. There is an understanding that we all have to agree on the kind of dog we finally decide to get. What are the chances of that? One member of our family, who shall remain nameless, has always wanted an Irish Setter, ever since she was a little girl way back in the 1950s. Another member of our family wants a Golden Retriever, I think perhaps to help her fetch cute boys. And the one who has been walking around with a leash in his hand, making plans for the doghouse, wants a Sharpei (you know, one of those wrinkly, crinkly Chinese dogs that looks like it's about a hundred and ten years old). And I want any kind of dog that will not shed hair on the couch, will not yip at me when I come home from work, and will not jump up and lick my face. I hate it when they do that.

So pray for us, especially if we ever do actually agree on what breed of dog to get. But, whatever you do, *don't* leave a puppy on our doorstep, because if you do I'll come over to your house and read what it says in Proverbs 26:17.

Like someone who takes a passing dog by the ears is one who meddles in the quarrels of another.

And if that has no effect, I'll say to you what the prophet Isaiah said to King Ahab:

Thus says the Lord, "In the place where dogs licked up the blood of Naboth, dogs will also lick up your blood."

You have been fairly warned.

Of The Soul

Laughter is one of the best cures for the winter blahs. It is one of the ways God lets light into our souls during the dog days of winter. But the dog days of the soul, the darkness we experience in the depth of our beings when we feel separated from the source of light, may require stronger medicine. Sometimes one can become so low, so depressed, that silliness and lighthearted fun cannot penetrate the darkness that engulfs the soul.

If you have ever been melancholy or depressed you know what I am talking about. Most of us experience depression at one time or another during our lives. Sometimes it lasts for a long time, and you may wonder if you will ever feel lighthearted again.

There are many causes for depression. It is wise to consult a physician to rule out physiological causes. Your symptoms may be treatable with light, vitamins or medication. It is also worth considering the possibility that God may be trying to tell you something. Your pain may be the beginning of a spiritual rebirth. Joan Borysenko, in her book *Fire in the Soul*, calls this unknown period "a necessary transition, like the transition period of labor, a natural process, not pathological." She says:

When our souls are on fire, old beliefs and opinions can be consumed, bringing us closer to our essential nature and to the heart of healing. These times of inner burning have been called dark nights of the soul. The Spanish mystic, St. John of the Cross, coined that term in the mid 1500's. He used it to designate that part of the spiritual journey during which we seem to lose our connection with an inner source of peace and instead confront our deepest fears and pains. St. John saw suffering as a "purgative" administered by the divine light to cleanse the soul of all residue that would keep it separate and alone.

(*Fire In the Soul,* Warner Books, 1993.)

It is terribly hard to cope when the light goes out of one's life. John says, "Those who do what is true come to the light."

It is up to us. We can receive the light into our lives or reject it. The light, which is our hope and salvation, is also a judgment. John says, "Those who believe in him are not condemned...." Indeed, he adds, "God did not send the Son into the world to condemn the world, but in order that the world might be saved through him." For it is as John assures us in that familiar verse which we read at the beginning of the text. Say it with me:

For God so loved the world that he gave his only Son, so that everyone who believes in him may not perish but may have eternal life.

Eternal light!

Author's note:

John shared this personal story about our dog search with the congregation at Wesley United Methodist Church in Kenosha, Wisconsin, in the winter of 1994. We adopted Eli, a West Highland Terrier (named for the priest who mentored Samuel), just after we moved to Wauwatosa in July of 1994. John and Eli are learning to live with each other.

Lent 5
Jeremiah 31:31-34

The Conversion

No longer shall they teach one another, or say to each other, "Know the Lord," for they shall all know me, from the least of them to the greatest, says the Lord; for I will forgive their iniquity, and remember their sin no more.
— verse 34

She hadn't intended to speak. In fact, she had thought she could sneak quietly into the church after the service began, sit in an inconspicuous place, and leave before it ended. She had no way of knowing before she got inside how open and exposed all of the seats in the small sanctuary were, not at all like the huge churches they showed in TV shows and movies. All she had meant to do was sit quietly and somehow communicate to God her thankfulness that her son had been spared. But she had felt exposed ever since she sat down. She was afraid everyone was looking and wondering, "What is *she* doing here?" And then the pastor had asked if anyone had concerns and celebrations to share, and before she could control herself she found her hand raised, just like she was in grade school again.

The pastor nodded at her, as nearly every eye in the church turned to look at her in the back pew. She swallowed to try and wet the inside of her mouth, where her tongue felt as if it were glued down. But, as she pulled herself to her feet, she saw the kind, welcoming eyes of the woman from the hospital several rows ahead, and she knew what to say.

"Most of you know my name is Mary Paul. I've lived in this town all of my life, and this is the first time I ever set foot in this church. My brothers and I have run the Whistle Stop tavern ever since our dad died. Our family never had anything to do with church. Dad used to say it was a conflict of interest."

A smile twitched the corner of her mouth, but she kept it from fully forming. The friendly woman nodded, though, and Mary kept going.

"I came in here today because I wanted to say thank you to God for the life of my son. I think you all know that Steve smashed up his car out on Highway 33 last Tuesday night. He's been in intensive care ever since, and they didn't give me much hope that he'd pull through. This morning at 7:00 they said he turned the corner, and they think he'll live. Up until Saturday morning, I would have only thought to thank the doctors that he pulled through. But on Saturday, a member of this church called on Steve and me at the hospital."

Some of the eyes of the congregation turned away from Mary at that point, and rested on the friendly face that still smiled softly at her. Mary pushed onward.

"I never met this woman before Saturday. I think she said her name is Eleanor, and I see her sitting over there. Well, Eleanor came into the waiting room when all my family and the people I call my friends had gone, and talked to me just like I was her friend. She said how sorry she was about Steve, and how she heard that the accident wasn't his fault, which is just the opposite of what everyone else was either saying or thinking. She asked if we could go into his room in the ICU together so she could say a prayer for him.

"I'm not one for praying. What my life has been like is no secret in this town. But she was so nice, and her caring was so real, that I said yes, and when she touched Steve's hand, with all those tubes and needles hooked in it, and prayed to God that he would be all right, well, I prayed that, too. I prayed for the first time I can remember in my whole life. And this morning they tell me Steve is going to pull through."

The lump in her throat, that had taken the place of the dryness, choked off most of her last words. She looked down, embarrassed, when tears escaped from her eyes and began to run down her face and nose. It just wasn't like her to cry over *anything*. Then she remembered the point she was trying to make, ignored the tears, and looked directly back at the congregation, most of whom now looked surprised.

"Anyhow," Mary said, "on my way home I saw all the cars here, and I just felt like I should come in and say thank you to God for my son's life. And while I'm at it, thank you, Eleanor, for being there at the right time for me and Steve. People like you are what goodness is really about. If there were more like you, maybe I would have been brave enough to come in here and say thanks to God sooner."

Then Mary Paul reached for her purse and keys on the pew and stepped out into the aisle to leave. But when she turned, Eleanor was standing beside her, and took her arm and led her forward to the pew where she had been sitting. And through the rest of the service they shared a bulletin and a hymnal and Christ's peace.

The Anointing

*His disciples did not understand these things at first; but
when Jesus was glorified, then they remembered that these
things had been written of him and had been done to him.*
— verse 16

Marilyn came slowly down the long stairs of her sister
Margaret's big brick house in the suburbs of Memphis. She could
see the rest of the dinner party already gathering at Margaret's well-
appointed dining room table. There were several steaming platters
of soul food: roast beef, collard greens, chitterlings, black-eyed
peas, cornbread and crisp fried chicken. Ralph was there with Jesse
and Andrew and several others less well-known, but very active in
the movement. And there was Martin, sitting at the head of the
table. What an honor it was to have him in their home again. They
had been friends for years, and he often stopped when he passed
through, but it was different now that he was an international figure.
To think, she was about to have dinner with the winner of the Nobel
Peace Prize. Marilyn wondered how he was handling all the media
attention. He seemed anxious when she talked to him on the phone
yesterday, concerned about the garbage workers' strike and fretting
about the violence that had broken out in the city before his arrival.
The words of his sermon at the church the night before still echoed
in her mind:

*We've got some difficult days ahead. But it doesn't matter
with me now. Because I've been to the mountaintop. And
I don't mind. Like anybody I would like to live a long life.
Longevity has its place. But I'm not concerned about
that now. I just want to do God's will.*

Was Martin's life in danger? No more than ever, he had assured them afterwards, but still the thought was always there in the backs of their minds. And that was why Marilyn was determined to give it to him tonight, before it was too late.

Leon met her at the bottom of the stairs. He had been acting as host, greeting everyone and showing them to their places at the table. If it weren't for Martin, her brother would be dead or in prison. There was no doubt in Marilyn's mind. Leon had been into drugs and was the leader of a gang for a while. Martin's invitation to join the movement had given him a purpose. He had found himself and was planning to go to law school.

"Hurry up," Leon said. "Everyone's waiting for you."

"I'll be there in a minute. I have to get something from the sewing room."

Marilyn entered the small room and picked up the quilt that she had been working on for over a year. Each embroidered panel showed a different scene from the movement: the bus strike in Montgomery, the marches in Birmingham and Selma, the words of Martin's "I Have a Dream" speech in front of the Lincoln Memorial in Washington, all lovingly depicted in bright-colored thread. Would he think it was too much? He would know how much work she had put into it. Martin had seen many of her quilts and had often complimented her on the artistry. "Your work will be in a museum someday," he had told her once. How could she not give him this quilt, the best of her craft, and inspired by his life?

Marilyn clutched the quilt tightly as she approached the table. Her hands trembled and her mouth tasted of cotton. She walked up behind Martin and wrapped the quilt around his shoulders. "Thank you," Marilyn said, "for all you have done." Tears streamed down her cheeks and dripped onto Martin's tie and his shirt as she hugged and kissed him.

There was a brief moment of awkward silence, and then applause as everyone got up and moved to embrace both of them. Marilyn heard later that one of the men had suggested to Martin that the quilt could be raffled off, and the money given to the families of the striking garbage collectors. But she knew it was only talk. Martin would never give the quilt away. He understood what it meant to her.

Marilyn was stunned the next day when she heard that Martin had been shot. She went into the sewing room and wept until she had no more tears.

Three days later, Marilyn watched as they carried Martin's casket up the street to his burial place. Her beautiful quilt covered one end of the casket. Oh, how glad she was that she had given it to him in time.

Author's note:

This story is historical fiction. Dr. Martin Luther King, Jr., was assassinated on April 4, 1968, at the Lorraine Motel in Memphis, Tennessee. He had come to Memphis to help settle the garbage workers' strike and to help bring a peaceful end to the violence which had erupted in some parts of the city. His co-workers in the Southern Christian Leadership Conference, Ralph Abernathy, Andrew Young and Jesse Jackson, were with him at the time he was shot. They were all getting ready to go out to a dinner of "soul food" at the home of The Reverend Samuel Kyles. The menu of this last meal prepared for Dr. King included roast beef, collard greens, chitterlings, black-eyed peas, cornbread and fried chicken. It was just the night before that Dr. King had delivered the now famous "Mountain Top" sermon at the Mason Temple, which included these words:

> *He's allowed me to go up to the mountain. And I've looked over. And I've seen the promised land. I may not get there with you. But I want you to know tonight, that we, as a people, will get to the promised land. And I am happy tonight. I'm not worried about anything. I'm not fearing any man. Mine eyes have seen the glory of the coming of the Lord.*

Mark Lane and Dick Gregory, *Murder in Memphis: The FBI and the Assassination of Martin Luther King* (New York: Thunder Mount Press, 1993), pp. 117-121.

Easter Sunday
John 20:1-18

Resurrection

Mary Magdalene went and announced to the disciples,
"I have seen the Lord."

— verse 18a

The first time I saw Maggie she was selling herself on the street like hundreds of other runaway teenagers I had seen before: small town, rural and suburban kids, lost in the big city, doing what they had to do to survive. For many of them this was better than what they had left behind. Stories of physical, emotional and sexual abuse were common, if you could get the kids to talk. Mostly it was what they didn't say, what the emptiness in their eyes revealed: deep hurt, unspeakable betrayals by fathers and mothers, uncles and aunts, grandpas and grandmas, teachers and pastors who should have protected them, should have loved them, but didn't. These were the used, abused and neglected of the world — throw-away kids in a throw-away society — the children whose experience had convinced them they were unloved and unlovable.

Our staff from the Abundant Life Center offered them hot coffee, sandwiches and a safe place to sleep if they wanted it. The van from the center was usually full by the time we had completed our nightly rounds. But some just took the coffee and the food and went straight back into the night. Maggie was one of those. We could never convince her to come back to the center. I don't know where she slept, maybe in the back of somebody's car or in the motel room where she turned her last trick.

There was one night when Maggie hung around the van for almost an hour. She seemed to need to talk, so I sat beside her on the curb and listened. She missed her brothers and sisters. Maggie was the second oldest of seven. She worried about her sisters. She had warned them about their dad and older brother, what they did when they got drunk. She had protected her sisters when she was at home, until she couldn't take it anymore. Her mom didn't seem to believe her, or was too frightened to do anything about it. She told a teacher at school and the pastor at her church, but neither of them believed her either. The pastor was one of her father's best friends. So she had just packed her bags and left. Nobody knew where she was and that was the way she was going to keep it. "I can take care of myself just fine," she said.

The next time I saw Maggie was on a cold Saturday night. I caught a glimpse of her as she started to cross the street at the intersection about two hundred yards from where the van was parked. I knew immediately that it was Maggie. You couldn't miss her. She had an unforgettable face, a rare beauty, and lush red hair besides. I called out her name, but she was too far away to hear. I had just turned away when I heard a screech of brakes and screams. I ran to see what had happened. Maggie's body was lying in the middle of the street. She didn't move when I touched her and she was barely breathing. I squeezed her hand. Maggie's eyes opened and she gave me a look of recognition. "Don't talk," I said, "I'll stay with you." I mouthed a prayer and I held her until the paramedics arrived.

I visited Maggie every day in the intensive care ward at the hospital. She was unconscious for almost a week. When she did come to, it was a long time before she was able to talk. It was after she was released from intensive care and moved to one of the rehab floors that we had our first real conversation since that night before the accident. She thanked me for staying with her. I was surprised when Maggie told me she remembered that I was there with her at the accident. I asked her if she wanted me to call her folks, but she said no thanks.

It was then that Maggie dropped the bombshell. "I saw Jesus," she said. At first I thought that I had misunderstood her. "He was with me in the ambulance," she went on. "Jesus called me by name, looked into my eyes and told me that he loved me. I wanted to go with him, but he said no, it wasn't my time yet and he needed me to stay here for a while. So I stayed."

Maggie smiled at me, as if she had just told me something quite ordinary. Then she squeezed my hand and said it was time for her

90

nap. Maggie never mentioned her strange vision again, but I could tell that she was a different person. There was a peace about her that was almost tangible. She had the glow of a small child who knows that she is adored by her parents, or that of a bride happily preparing for her wedding. For the first time in her life, Maggie knew that she was loved.

Maggie and I lost touch for several months after she got out of the hospital. Then, one day, I spotted her on a street corner in the same neighborhood where we met. She was surrounded by a small group of street kids, some of her old friends. I was disappointed at first. What was she doing back here? I had hoped that she had found a better life for herself. Had she forgotten her vision?

Maggie picked up a guitar that had been leaning against the street light. As she began to play and sing in a soft, sweet voice, I knew that her transformation had been complete. My soul soared as I listened, enthralled by her music:

I am the resurrection, I am the life - He who believes in me shall never die; Jesus is calling to you, looking in your eyes. Do you believe? Do you believe?

Author's Note:

Lyrics and music to "I Am The Resurrection" by Cheryl Kirking Kilker. Reprinted by permission. Cheryl's tapes and CD's are available from Mill Pond Music, PO Box 525, Lake Mills, WI 53551. The story was inspired by Cheryl's song.

Friends

---

*How very good and pleasant it is when kindred live
together in unity! It is like the precious oil on the head,
running down upon the beard, on the beard of Aaron,
running down over the collar of his robes. It is like the
dew of Hermon, which falls on the mountains of Zion.
For there the Lord ordained his blessing, life forevermore.*
— Psalm 133

Marty pulled into the crowded hospital parking lot and began
her daily ritual search for a parking space. She turned up one aisle,
down the next, her expert eyes peeled for an empty spot, taillights,
or the telltale exhaust of a recently started engine. It had been a
long, long day at work, and she didn't really want to be here. There
was laundry piled up at home, the dishes hadn't been done the
night before, and the refrigerator was nearly empty; the kids would
be home from school, unsupervised, for about half an hour, again,
but she knew it would all wait. Although it had been almost a year,
with no sign of change or hope, she was compelled to come and sit
with him. Some part of her soul that transcended reason brought
her back every day.

"He's my brother," she thought defensively as she waited for a
small white Buick to back out in front of her, then maneuvered her
much larger minivan into the narrow space. "All we have left is
each other." A wave of melancholy rolled over her, along with the
cold March wind off the lake, as she left the warmth of the car and
joined the straggling procession of visitors to the hospital entrance.
It was so hard to see him this way ... dead to everything outside
himself, but breathing, his heart beating as strong as ever, and, she
believed, alive in his mind.

The doctors refused to give her false hope. They insisted that
his brain was alive, but they would not predict when or if the coma,

brought on by the high fever that had accompanied a bout of meningitis, would end. They encouraged her to talk to him, play music he liked, read to him, because there was no certainty that he couldn't hear everything going on around him. Still, they would not say that he would recover. Their job was to keep his body nourished, exercised and functioning to the best of their abilities. Hers was to keep the vigil. After nearly 10 months, it grew more and more difficult every day.

As she entered the hospital, and nodded to the familiar security people and receptionist before she turned into the nursing home hallway, she wondered why that part down deep inside her wouldn't let go. When their parents were killed while she and Russ were still small, she hadn't wanted to let go. She hadn't wanted to accept it when they were teens and their grandmother died of a stroke, forcing them to move in with one set of aunts and uncles after another until both of them had graduated from high school. But, in both cases, she had let go. There had been no real choice. This time was different. Marty had come to believe that it was because, down deep in her soul, she knew Russ would live. She was the only one left to care ... she and ....

Marty walked toward the elevator, thinking of Jack, Russ' best friend, and feeling a familiar anger that he had not come to visit in all of these months. She was astounded when she looked up and saw Jack standing at the end of the hall, as if he were waiting for her. The look on his face and the pain in his eyes melted her anger, and she ran the remaining distance and threw her arms around him.

"Oh, Jack! I'm so glad you came! Please, come up with me and talk to him."

"I thought he was in a coma," Jack replied, and she drew back as if repelled by his words.

"The doctors say talking to him is good. His brain is still alive. He could wake up. Maybe you can get through to him."

As they rode to the third floor on the elevator, she related to him the pain of her months of waiting, hoping, giving up and hoping again. She told him, in words, what had been done to keep Russ' body functioning, but words could not prepare Jack for the sight of his friend, pale and thin, hooked up to numerous machines and tubes, and looking much more like death than life.

"Russ, I'm here!" Marty announced, pulling Jack to the bedside, though he resisted slightly. "Someone else has come to visit you, too. I wish you could see him. I know you'd jump all over one another and whoop and yell. Jack is here, Russ. Can't you please wake up and say hi to Jack?"

There was a brief moment of anticipation for both of them — she holding Jack's hand as he hung back, as much to comfort herself as to keep him in his place at the bedside. But the moment passed and there was no movement from the hospital bed but the steady rise and fall of Russ' chest.

Marty brushed away angry tears. "Why do I do that? Why do I get so hopeful when I should know there is no hope?"

Jack put his arm around her shoulder and pulled her close, handing her a tissue from the box on the bedside table. Seeing Russ this way was every bit as bad as he had imagined it would be. That was what had kept him away. He had wanted to come, but he hadn't been able to bear the sight. He still couldn't. Jack wiped away his own tears as he comforted Marty. It seemed to be the most he could do for Russ at this point, as the memories of their childhood flooded in. So he pulled a chair into place beside the bed, where Marty perched herself next to her brother, and he said to her as he sat down, "Do you remember the Halloween Russ and I got busted for egging old lady Miller's picture window?"

What followed was an outpouring of loving remembrances, punctuated by laughter, sprinkled with tears, directed from Marty and Jack to one another and to Russ as he lay near them and came alive to them again in their stories. Finally, when the tales exhausted themselves, Marty became somber again.

"It hurt so much when you didn't come after I called you. We both needed you. There isn't anyone else. Bill doesn't understand why I still come everyday. The kids are too young. I know it's not true, but I keep thinking that maybe if you had come sooner, he would have come out of it. I guess I'm just frustrated because he won't wake up for me. Every morning I get up and tell myself, no more! I'm not going to go there and put myself through it all again.

96

But every night, after work, here I am. My house is a disaster, dinner is always late, the kids are alone after school, and it's straining my marriage. The doctors say any little thing could suddenly bring him out of the coma, but they won't really give me any hope that it will actually happen, and still I can't stop coming! What I wonder is, after all this time, what made you come?"

Jack tried to swallow the lump in his throat, and his eyes filled with tears again as he forced his gaze away from Russ' almost lifeless form to Marty's red-rimmed eyes. At first all he could manage was a shrug, but finally he cleared his throat and said softly, "There's a part of me that can't let go. Just like you said you can't stop coming, I couldn't stop thinking about coming, even though I didn't want to. There's this old song that keeps going through my head, day after day. I think we learned it at camp or something. Do you remember it?" And he sang softly:

"Friends, I will remember you, think of you, pray for you.
And when another day is through, I'll still be friends with you."

His voice cracked on the final line, and Marty burst into tears again. There was a long silence. The hand that reached out and covered Marty's to comfort her felt stiff when her hand closed around it in response. She looked up, in shock, at Russ, whose eyes gazed back in love, first at her, and then at Jack, as he whispered hoarsely, "I'm thirsty."

The Pine Lake Creaker

Jesus himself stood among them and said to them, "Peace be with you." They were startled and terrified, and thought they were seeing a ghost.

— verses 36b-37

I am going to tell you one of the little-known stories in the history of Pine Lake Camp. It happened a long, long time ago, when Don Mevis still had most of his hair, just a couple of years after the twenty-fifth anniversary of the camp. It is the story of "The Pine Lake Creaker."

It was a crisp, moonlit night, about this time of year. I remember it well because it was my first visit to Pine Lake and it was the week before Jo and I were married. I was counseling in Birchwood 3 with a group of six junior high boys. The week had gone pretty well. We were over the hump. It was Thursday night. We had had a long day of hiking around the lake, volleyball, a water carnival in the afternoon and, to cap it all off, a picnic supper and campfire out on the point. We told stories and sang songs around the fire until almost eleven o'clock. By the time I got the campers back to the cabin and into their sleeping bags it was nearly midnight, and we were all exhausted. At least, that's what I thought. It was then that I made a foolish, rookie counselor's mistake. I went to sleep before they did. I had yet to learn about the residual effects of s'mores and what we used to call Pine Lake bug juice. You mix four or five s'mores with a gallon or two of that high octane bug juice and pour it all into a post-pubescent camper with all of those raging adolescent hormones and you've got something truly dangerous. Six of them together in one cabin is an apocalypse waiting to happen. I know that now, after twenty-four years of counseling, and if I had that night to live over again, you can be sure that I would have bolted the cabin door and insisted on a long period of scriptural devotions.

98

I could have read through First and Second Chronicles and maybe a few chapters of Deuteronomy and Leviticus, slowly, deliberately, in a quiet, meditative voice. This would have been followed by thirty or forty minutes of silent prayer. But I didn't think of that then, and to this day I cringe when I think about the consequences of my foolish negligence. What those young campers heard and saw on that fateful night has haunted me all these years. I can only now bring myself to speak of it.

I must have wakened when they closed the cabin door. There was a squeak in the hinges, and as quiet as they tried to be, they couldn't muffle that squeak. It took me only a few moments to realize that I was alone. There was a conspicuous absence of heavy breathing. I looked out the window in time to see the last boy disappearing around the corner of the trail. I jumped into my pants and set off after them. They stopped down by the shower house and began to confer among themselves. I ducked down behind some bushes, thinking I would sneak up on them and give them a good scare. As I drew closer, I overheard them plotting to raid one of the girls' cabins at the top of the hill. I listened long enough to catch the gist of their plans, and then I turned and made my way quickly back to the cabin. There was just enough time to give them a scare they would never forget. I took down the clothesline and grabbed the sheet out of my sleeping bag. I wrapped a pillow in one end of the sheet, tied it off with the rope and headed up the path ahead of the boys, looking for a low limb from which to hang my surprise. I found one around the bend, about a hundred yards from the girls' cabin. I threw the rope over the limb, adjusted the height, practiced raising and lowering it a few times, and then sat back to wait. It wasn't long before I heard them coming noisily up the path. I heard somebody whisper "shhh," and they became very quiet as they approached the bend. I was just about to drop the surprise and yell, "Boooo," in my best ghostly voice, when suddenly, out of the darkness, came the most unearthly sound I have ever heard. Creeeeeeek! It was bone-chilling. The boys stopped dead in their tracks, their faces turned pale in the moonlight. And then it came again, in a lower key, floating out on the mist that hung low over the lake and echoing back again. Creaaaaaaaaaaaak! It sounded like the lamentations of some long lost soul, murdered perhaps by early Methodists in the Pine Lake woods, come back now to seek its ghastly revenge.

We listened and waited, and when the Creaker moaned again, to my great horror, the boys set off after it, straight through the woods. The sound seemed to have a hypnotic effect on them, pulling them along mindlessly, like zombies fresh from the grave. I trailed along behind, drawn with them toward the source of the Creeeeeeeek!

We came out of the woods by the nurse's cabin and headed up the driveway above the lodge. I could tell the Creaker was near now. The sounds were coming closer and closer together, one after another Creeeeeeeeek! Creaaaaaaaaaak! We were led around to the back of the big house on the hill above the lodge. And then we saw it through the trees, perched on the deck that had been built out over the garage. It had great hairy legs and a shiny spot on the top of its head which seemed to glow in the moonlight. Creeeeeeek! Creaaaaaaaak! We watched and listened for several minutes and then suddenly the Creaker rose up on its haunches and let out a deep gutteral roar. Aaaaahgggggg! The boys screamed and took off running back to the cabin as fast as their legs could carry them, shrieking and whimpering all the way.

I was petrified at first, but still curious enough to want to get a good look at the creature. I drew nearer to the deck, hoping to get a better look at the Creaker before it disappeared into the night. When I saw it clearly, I couldn't believe my eyes. It was Don Mevis, the camp manager! He had on an old pair of Pine Lake shorts and a scruffy T-shirt with big black letters that read "World's Greatest Camp Manager." He was sitting in his rocking chair, sipping from a frothy mug of Pine Lake kool-aid, that special brew they mix up just for the staff, and looking out over his kingdom. Every time he rocked forward the chair went Creeeeeeeeek! And when he rocked backwards, it went Creaaaaaaaaaak! I watched for a few moments, until I saw Creaker's head drop and I heard him begin to snore (Agghhhhhh).

Not a word was spoken about the events of that night in our cabin the following morning, or at any other time during the rest of that week.

As for the Creaker, he still lives in the big house on the hill above the lodge. The deck over the garage has been closed in to make a large recreation room with a hot tub. Now, on moonlit nights, the only sounds that can be heard in the camp are great contented sighs and happy sloshing as the Creaker cavorts in the hot tub with his lovely wife, Elaine, and sometimes guests from the Executive Committee of the Conference Board of Camp and Retreat Ministries, of which I am a longtime member.

Author's Note:

Donald Mevis is Manager/Director of Pine Lake United Methodist Camp near Westfield, Wisconsin. On August 21, 1993, John told this story at the 45th anniversary celebration of the camp and presented Don with a T-shirt with lettering which read "THE WORLD'S GREATEST CAMP MANAGER."

Surely Goodness And Mercy ...

Even though I walk through the darkest valley, I fear no evil; for you are with me; your rod and your staff — they comfort me. You prepare a table before me in the presence of my enemies; you anoint my head with oil; my cup overflows. Surely goodness and mercy shall follow me all the days of my life, and I shall dwell in the house of the Lord my whole life long.

— verses 4-6

As a child psychologist, I have the privilege of meeting and speaking with a great many people. I work with children, adolescents, and their parents, but it is almost always some adult who has decided the child or teenager should see me. It is rarely the minor's initiative. And, because of where I have chosen to work, most of my clients are not only forced to see me, they are usually black as well. That is no small issue, given that I am white and solidly suburban in lifestyle. I am not, nor have I ever been, poor. Since I work in urban hospitals and county mental centers, the vast majority of my clients are impoverished. In short, I am as different from my clients as I could possibly be, and I have tried to use that to my advantage whenever I could. As I inform them, and enlighten them, I am aware that they will also inform and enlighten me. The street runs two ways, and I hope they will feel some equity in the arrangement, and, therefore, be more comfortable with it. I, with some ten years of college, have learned a lot from children and teenagers. In the summer of 1990, a young man came to see me, sent by his probation officer, and he taught me a great deal. I will never forget him, or others like him. They haunt me.

Strangely, I do not remember his name. He was sixteen or so, and after that one appointment, he never came back. But for that one morning, he tolerated me. He sat in my office and answered my questions. He was big, and tough, and black. He wore a long coat, even though it was summer, and I think he had a gun under it. He rode to my office hidden under a blanket in the back of a car because my place was in an unfriendly neighborhood. If the wrong people saw him, they would try to kill him. He was a felon, and his probation officer told him he had to see me. In the interest of a lenient sentence, he complied. I'm not sure what I was supposed to do for him, but I was willing to meet him and hear his story.

He lumbered into my office, and his huge body filled the small chair to overflowing. He was well over six feet tall and looked to weigh about 250 pounds. I, a neatly dressed professional, and he, the apparent epitome of a black thug, made quite a pair. We struck up our conversation, and within the first few minutes he revealed to me that he wanted to be a drug dealer; he wanted to make a lot of easy money — he wanted to be rich. For the next half hour, our conversation was like a contest: two boxers circling, feeling for weaknesses and strengths. He answered as I expected, and I asked just what I was supposed to ask. Nothing of any import was revealed. But, for some strange reason that I do not understand, though it has happened again since, we slowly dropped our guard. As more than an hour passed, we almost forgot who we were. The walls slid down, and his spirit was revealed. While I could not have recognized it at the time, it was a beautiful thing.

I repeated an earlier question and asked this new person before me what he wanted to be in life, what he wanted to do: what were his hopes and his dreams? This hulking man-child, armed and hidden behind shades, leaned back in his seat, tilted his head, held his arms out and up in the way people do when they make a plea, and cried, "I want to be a doctor. I've always wanted to be a doctor for as long as I can remember." Tears rolled out from under his sunglasses and down his cheeks and etched themselves into my mind.

"Yeah," I said, not at all meaning what I was about to say, "that's a good job. Doctors make a lot of money." He shot straight up and screamed out loud when he heard my words. The tears poured down his face and his body heaved in that way people's do when they cry uncontrollably, like they can't get air. He reacted as though my words had stabbed him.

"That ain't it!" he bellowed. "Doctors help people. I wanna help people. But now that ain't gonna happen. I'm never gonna be a doctor, not anymore." He truly believed, at sixteen, that his dreams were dead. As we talked, I came to know that he had decided by the age of twelve that he could never become a doctor: that no one would let him be a physician after all the trouble he had been in.

I know now that he had spent his young life struggling upstream against a terrible current ... as though he had been born into a river, and everywhere he wanted to go lay in the opposite direction from where the current was trying to take him. At that moment, when he was 12, he let go his grip and slipped off into the current. It washed him so far downstream, so fast, that I am certain his dreams were lost in the distance before that day was over. Though he was smart enough, and once good enough, he could not hang on against the pressure of the current. The river had not killed him yet, but it had hollowed him out, and now life beat his hollow body for a drum.

As I reflect on things, I can see that my life has been, largely, an effortless drift within a different current. It's as though, at my birth, I was set into a different river, and I have been carried along by the flow of that stream ever since. I drifted through the turns and eddies, confident that the river would carry me to not one, but many satisfying points and destinations. Any minor snag was rectified with little effort. A small push, and I was on my way again. I had absolute faith that the river would be kind, that my best interests would be served. The current held achievement and success for me. All I had to do was drift.

How different my life has been from that young man's, and others like him. If you are young and black, and especially if you are poor as well, you will be born into a river where the current is not your friend. It carries you to places you do not want to go, and away from places you long desperately to visit. To reach your goals, your destinations, you must struggle against the current. You must swim and kick and claw against unrelenting forces directed away from your dreams. For so many, the current is not their friend, but their enemy. As it pushes against their bodies, and tears at their souls, it also whispers in their ears and begs them to give up.

Many do give up. They let go their handholds and set themselves into the river. They relax and wash downstream as their dreams sink below the vanishing horizon behind them. As they rest, freed from the struggle, it is their dreams that drown first, long before their bodies. The distance to their goals grows vast, and they remake themselves in a new image. They take on the goals of the murderous current. They deceive themselves in the name of rest and embrace certain doom as though it was their true destination all along. They pretend they want to go to the only place the current will take them. My young friend let go when he was twelve — some last longer, others do not.

Late in that summer of 1990, another teenager taught me how easy it is to hurt someone, even someone I would never meet.

Just a few weeks after that first young man shared his withered dreams with me, another young man came through my office door. He was older, and tougher, too. He never warmed to me, though I tried to thaw him out. There was no moment of relaxation; I never felt any closer to him than I did at that moment he came into the room. Still, he was honest and open — more so than I necessarily deserved. He described his alcoholic father and his mother on cocaine. He told me about his younger sister who had sex with too many men, and he described the multiple crimes and doings of his gang life. I asked him what was the worst experience of his life, what stuck out as the one thing that hurt him most. I had no right to this information, but he gave it to me anyway. He did not cry as he answered, but neither did he hesitate. He knew precisely what it was, and he related it to me in detail so complete and poignant that I will never forget it.

One evening, near dusk, he and some friends walked down the block in front of his house. It was a good neighborhood, and the sun was still up some. The boys were loud and active, like boys always are in summer. At the end of the block, from the direction they were going, came a woman with a baby in a stroller. He did not notice her, but she noticed them. When they reached her, she screamed. Though they had said nothing to her, and no one had touched her in any way, she offered them money if they would agree not to hurt her or her baby. She dug in her purse and held out the few dollars she had, hoping that she could protect herself and her child from attack.

Because they were young, and black, and loud, she assumed they would hurt her, and her infant, too. That young man burned inside when he remembered that night. "I wasn't gonna hurt her. I wouldn't hurt no woman, or a baby," he said. Nothing else ever cut him like that woman's fear. It had been more than a year since it happened, but he would never forget it. He felt he could help his father, his mother, and his sister. He could see what he might do in those cases. But what would he do about people he didn't even know who were afraid of him? The world was filled with people he would never meet who would die fearing him just because he was black and young. Their fear added itself to the current in his river and pounded him like a hammer.

If I had already learned the importance of dreams to the soul, he taught me how easy it is to hurt someone else. All you have to do is be afraid of them. Fear someone, and you can sting them where they can't fight back. I am convinced that fear makes up a great deal of the current that bears down on them in that other river. My fear and the fears of others somehow add together to make the river deadly. To know that others fear you because of who you are is a terrible thing. It tore that boy's heart to shreds, and he spent much of his time convincing himself that he never had a heart in the first place. How odd, that the frightened would turn out to be so dangerous, that the way of things would reveal our fears to be lethal. As I drift down my current, I try to give up my fears, hoping that I might lessen the burden somewhere, on someone.

Author's Note:

These stories and reflections come from Dr. Steven Dykstra, a child psychologist with the Milwaukee County Child and Adolescent Treatment Center. He teaches the Senior High Sunday School class at Wauwatosa Avenue United Methodist Church in Wauwatosa, Wisconsin.

Summer Fruit

---

*"Abide in me as I abide in you. Just as the branch cannot
bear fruit by itself unless it abides in the vine, neither can
you unless you abide in me. I am the vine, you are the
branches. Those who abide in me and I in them bear much
fruit, because apart from me you can do nothing."*
— verses 4-5

There was once a pastor who served a very active congregation;
that is to say, they were active most of the year. Throughout the
fall, winter and spring, the church was full every Sunday. There
were several choirs which sang on a regular basis. There were many
children, youth and adults in Sunday School, and their mission
organization was the envy of all of the surrounding churches. They
had programs to feed the hungry, house the homeless, comfort the
bereaved, visit the sick, and a special prayer ministry with prisoners
in the local jail. There was just one thing lacking in this seemingly
vital congregation — only a few hearty souls came to worship in
the summer. And those who did come were there quite irregularly.
Many of the young families stayed away all summer. On most
Sundays, only one or two small children came up to the chancel
during the Children's Moment.

This troubled the pastor, because the church seemed to die after
Memorial Day; and every year it took longer and longer for it to
come alive again after Labor Day. When he asked the leaders why
worship attendance was so sparse in the summertime, they told
him that it had always been that way. "Our church doesn't do much
in the summer. People are traveling or at their cottages up at the
lake. The kids have been in school all winter, so parents like to give
them a break in the summertime. Don't worry, everyone will be
back in the fall." But the pastor did worry. He knew that when
members of the body of Christ are absent from worship for more

than one or two weeks, the ministry of the whole church is greatly diminished. Jesus' words in John's Gospel came into his mind, "Those who abide in me and I in them bear much fruit, because apart from me you can do nothing."

The pastor felt he had a responsibility to do something, but he didn't know what. Then one spring, after much prayer and several sleepless nights, he had an inspiration. He would recommend to the board that they have worship just once a month in the summer, and that the service be held on Wednesday evenings so that weekends would be free for family outings. Then no one would have to feel guilty about missing worship. About a week before the board meeting, the pastor sent a letter to all of the members outlining his plan. When it came time for the meeting, the church was packed. They had to move the proceedings into the sanctuary. After the pastor moved his recommendation for the new summer worship schedule, several irate members got up, one after the other, to speak against the plan. Why, they had never heard of such a thing! Not have worship on Sundays? It was positively unchristian! When the vote was taken, the pastor's proposal was unanimously defeated.

The pastor didn't comment, but when they asked him to pray at the end of the meeting he stood up and said, "How many of you plan to be in worship this summer?" The startled members of the congregation looked at each other with surprise in their eyes. Slowly, one by one, they raised their hands. Then the pastor bowed his head and prayed, "O Lord, thank you for the faithfulness of this congregation."

That summer, and each summer after, the church was full every Sunday.

Dorothy's Story

---

*"As the Father has loved me, so I have loved you; abide
in my love. If you keep my commandments, you will abide
in my love, just as I have kept my Father's commandments
and abide in his love. I have said these things to you so
that my joy may be in you, and that your joy may be
complete."*

— verses 9-11

One evening, when I was 26 years old, beleagered by guilt for
acknowledged sins, I was deep into an hour-long prayer of
repentance. In despair, I grieved that I had broken the
commandments and that I was not worthy of God's love.

Near me lay the Bible, unused and unfamiliar. I had never, ever
read from the Bible. Yet my hands reached out and took the Bible
to open it. I knew not where, nor why. But my hands knew the way.
They opened to John 15:9-11 and as my eyes began to read, my
mind knew the meaning with clarity. My eyes read verse 10 first:

*"If ye keep my commandments, ye shall abide in my love;
even as I have kept my Father's commandments, and abide
in his love."*

Next I saw verse 9:

*"As the Father has loved me, so have I loved you: Continue
ye in my love."*

Then I continued with verse 11:

*"These things I have spoken to you that my joy might
remain in you, and your joy might be complete."*

Even as I was assimilating this message, I became distinctly aware of a Presence. I marveled at this feeling and my awareness became intense. Fearing that the Presence would not be real, I dared to lift my eyes from the Bible. The Presence remained and lifted my spirit until I felt an inner gladness that was wonderful.

The Presence itself was vague and human-size. I could not see it, though I looked directly at it and knew it was there. The effect of the Presence was all around me.

Still testing the reality, I looked at the Bible and read the verses of John 15:9-11 again. I tried to read verses 12 and 13 or verse 8, then verse 12 again, but those words were blurred to my vision. My eyes could see only verses 9, 10 and 11, so I reread these verses again in the order they had been presented to me, to accept and instill what I recognized as an answer to my prayers. And still the Presence was around me, absolute. *I knew it was Jesus, absolutely.*

My perception of the Presence remained with me for several minutes after Jesus was gone. My conception of joy was sustained.

This event changed my life. I never again have questioned whether I am forgiven. I feel secure in God's love. I trust the Spirit of Jesus' presence. I believe and trust in prayer. I try to have my prayers include listening. I live life with a comprehension of the wonder.

As I have read and studied the Bible in the many years beyond this episode, the same message seems clearly evident for all who read to see, for those who pray to know, and for all who love to be.

Through some years of spiritual drought, when I searched in vain for relief in prayer, and through a long depression, when I liked myself less and less, I never did lose my faith. That in itself is part of the wonder. I remembered the Presence I knew and the gift message I had received.

We can know God loves us. We can trust God hears our prayers. We can feel the presence of Jesus, and so we can live in joy.

Author's note:
Dorothy Kraemer was a long-time, faithful member of Wauwatosa Avenue United Methodist Church in Wauwatosa,

Wisconsin. This story, written in her own words, was read at her memorial service at the church on September 1, 1995. On July 13, a few weeks before her death, she wrote of the moon she had observed that evening through the window by her hospital bed:

> ... a couple of hours later the moon was still there, lower in the sky, and paled, yet ever so serene, still watching, always watching me. Or was it a lifetime that had passed in the night? And the moon represented our lives gone by together? If that is so, the end is near because a dawning blue was creeping into the heaven. It would not be long now. I looked at the low hanging moon and marveled at its peace. Then I fell asleep.

The Ascension Of Our Lord
Luke 24:44-53

Witnesses

Then he opened their minds to understand the scriptures, and he said to them, "Thus it is written, that the Messiah is to suffer and to rise from the dead on the third day, and that repentance and forgiveness of sins is to be proclaimed in his name to all nations, beginning from Jerusalem. You are witnesses of these things."

— verses 45-48

There was a young couple in a small country church who had a very beautiful little daughter who was a favorite of everyone in the congregation. Clarissa had golden hair and was pretty and bright, with a sweet disposition. Ardella liked to dress her up in frilly dresses and bonnets when they came to church. Everyone loved to fuss over little Clarry, as her father called her. Gilbert used to take her fishing down by the river, and they would laugh together at the antics of the muskrats and the beaver they saw playing along the banks.

Then, one day, they discovered that Clarissa had a fast-growing, malignant tumor on her brain. The tumor was inoperable and untreatable. Clarissa died four months later, exactly a week before her fifth birthday. Gilbert picked up Clarissa's lifeless body and carried her across the long river bridge, all the way to the funeral parlor in town. Ardella and Gilbert remained faithful to the church, but the light had gone out of their lives. Everyone in the congregation grieved with them. After several months, it was apparent that both of them were deeply depressed. They talked to the pastor; they went to a therapist for counseling, but nothing seemed to help.

One Sunday morning, almost two years to the day after Clarissa's death, Gilbert and Ardella came into the church with smiles on their faces. Everyone could tell that something had happened, but they didn't know what. Gilbert and Ardella just said it had something to do with a gift of the Spirit. It wasn't until several months later that the congregation finally heard the full story.

There was an old Jehovah's Witness couple who had been coming to witness to Gilbert and Ardella for several years. They never turned them away, even though they were not much interested in the old couple's religion. Gilbert and Ardella would listen politely and sometimes they would share a little of their own faith. After the couple's religious obligation was completed, Ardella would always insist that they stay and visit a while. Then she would lead them into the kitchen for milk and fresh bread with homemade strawberry jam. Often there was hot soup on the stove to go with the bread. They visited about everyday concerns, sometimes laughing and talking until late in the afternoon, well past chore time. When Clarissa died, the old couple came more often and said little about their religion.

Gilbert and Ardella noticed one day that it had been several months since the couple's last visit, and they began to wonder what had happened to them. They had never exchanged last names or telephone numbers. Gilbert and Ardella had no idea where the old couple lived or how to contact them. All they could do was wait and wonder. Several months passed, and then, one day, the old man showed up on their front doorstep alone. He said his wife had died quite suddenly, and he had been so grief-stricken that he had not been able to get out to do his witnessing. Gilbert invited him in, and Ardella made him sit down and have some soup with them. As he told about his wife's death, they wept with him, and put their arms around him, and loved him.

Easter 7
John 17:6-19

A Mother's Prayer

---

*"I have made your name known to those whom you gave
me from the world. They were yours, and you gave them
to me, and they have kept your word. Now they know that
everything you have given me is from you; for the words
that you gave to me I have given to them, and they have
received them and know in truth that I came from you;
and they have believed that you sent me. I am asking on
their behalf; I am not asking on behalf of the world, but
on behalf of those whom you gave me, because they are
yours. All mine are yours, and yours are mine; and I have
been glorified in them. And now I am no longer in the
world, but they are in the world, and I am coming to you.
Holy Father, protect them in your name that you have
given me, so that they may be one, as we are one. While I
was with them, I protected them in your name that you
have given me. I guarded them, and not one of them was
lost except the one destined to be lost, so that the scripture
might be fulfilled. But now I am coming to you, and I
speak these things in the world so that they may have joy
made complete in themselves. I have given them your
word, and the world has hated them because they do not
belong to the world, just as I do not belong to the world.
I am not asking you to take them out of the world, but I
ask you to protect them from the evil one."*

— verses 6-15

It was the same every night when Ruth Kristmon got into her
bed. First she thought of Ray, her late husband, who had laid beside
her in the very same bed for 49 years and three months, until his
death the previous spring. "I'm coming home soon, Ray," Ruth
always said. "I'll meet you in All Saints Park under the Tenth Street
bridge." This favorite memory of their courting days, their secret

114

meetings under the bridge, brought a smile to her lips. And then Ruth's thoughts always turned to their children.

"Lord, be with Peter. Give him strength for his work. He has looked so tired and discouraged lately. I wish I was able to help him like I used to when I was able to drive the car. I don't think he has been eating regularly or getting enough sleep. Help him to slow down, Lord. Let him know that he is not the only one working in your world. You know how I worry, Lord. I just don't want Peter to end up with an ulcer like his uncle, Paul.

"Bless Andy, dear Lord, my sweet traveling son. The work you give him takes him so far away. I miss looking upon his face and hearing him laugh. No one can make me laugh like Andy. What a gift you have given him. I worry about him being out on the highway so much. And be with Sally and their children. My heart still aches for Sally. She hasn't come around much since their divorce. I know I have to accept it, Lord, but I don't have to like it. I wish they could be together again. I know Andy needs her and I think he is beginning to know it, too. Keep Andy safe, Lord. Bring him home soon.

"And Steven, dead now these thirty years. How my heart longs for him. I have trusted Steven to your care, Lord. It was the only way I could go on. It was so hard to see his life cut short. I wish it had been me who took the stand instead of him. Perhaps I wouldn't have been as much of a threat to them. But then, it was his work to do, and it was for your glory. I have to accept that, too. Will I see Steven again? Will he be there to meet me, too? Surely he will. I can see him there with Ray, his arm on his dad's shoulder and that cock-eyed grin.

"Thank you for Mary, Lord. How blessed I am to have a daughter like her. If only you hadn't made us so much alike, it might have been easier for us. It's better now that her children are grown. We seem to have come to an understanding. How good it is to see her every day. I don't tell her enough how much I appreciate her. I'm afraid I complain too much about my own aches and pains. Do I expect too much of her, Lord? Don't let Mary overdo on my account. Let her enjoy a life of her own, too.

"And John, O Lord, how proud I am of John. I wish I could visit him more often. Letters seem inadequate to convey all the love we all have for him. Set him free, Lord. You know, as I know, that he is innocent. You know that if he had pleaded guilty he would have been free by now. But John is not of this world. I taught him too well to love truth and to give himself for others. He would have died before he would have implicated the friend he knew to be innocent, too. Keep him safe from all the evil in that place, O Lord. And if it be your will, bring him home to me, a free man, before I die."

Ruth's prayer went on for almost an hour, as it did every night before she went to sleep. She remembered each of her children, their spouses, her seventeen grandchildren and David and Melissa, her new great-grandchildren. "Bless all my babies," Ruth prayed. "Keep them safe, every one."

Pentecost
Acts 2:1-21

Prejudice, Once Removed:
The Larry Wasson Story

When the day of Pentecost had come, they were all together in one place. And suddenly from heaven there came a sound like the rush of a violent wind, and it filled the entire house where they were sitting. Divided tongues, as of fire, appeared among them, and a tongue rested on each of them. All of them were filled with the Holy Spirit and began to speak in other languages, as the Spirit gave them ability.
— verses 1-4

The gray-haired man cleared his throat and stood before the circle of his peers, gathered to share their stories.

"My story is a little bit different," he said, smiling at the woman who had just put an effectively humorous ending on her story. "It's a story of how insidiously easy it is to instill racial bias in the lives of people ... particularly young people."

His southern drawl eased into a quiet, soothing tone as he became comfortable with his tale. "I was born and raised in a little coal mining town in the foothills of the Ozarks in Arkansas. And one of the high points of the history of this little town, its sense of its importance, was a simple statement that floated around the community almost like an ambiance; and that statement was: 'No nigger ever stayed overnight in this town.'

"My parents didn't particularly promote that statement. They were neutral about it, and I thought that I was not affected by it. I thought that I was fairly free of any kind of prejudice. I grew up, went on to high school and college. In college, the janitor in our dormitory was a negro, liked and respected by everyone on campus, including me. So, I went on assuring myself that I was free of any kind of racial bias.

"After we married, my wife and I came to Milwaukee, and in due course, we became chairpersons of the Commission on

117

Christian Social Concerns in our church. As a part of our responsibility to the commission, my wife suggested that maybe it would be a good idea for us to visit one of the African-American United Methodist churches in Milwaukee. I agreed to it without any major reservations.

"So, one Sunday morning we went down to one of the black neighborhoods. We parked our car and walked over to the church, about a block away. And I found myself struck by a tremendous sense of dread. It's nothing I can put a name to, even now. It was just a dread I felt of going into that church. It amazed me, because I still didn't think of myself as prejudiced. But if I had had any kind of excuse with which I could have saved face, I would have turned around and gone back home."

He shook his head, then, and rubbed his chin as if in disbelief, even yet, of those very real feelings. Then he smiled. "But my wife didn't let that happen! She took my arm and we went on into that church, where we were accepted like long-lost kinfolk.

"Well, that's the story of how I became aware of the fact that I had been tainted by the racism I grew up with: that I had carried around an internal bias that I had not even been conscious of. The blessing is that I got over it.

"Having a spotlight shone on something in yourself that you don't like is very helpful in taking steps to remedy it. One thing I did was to sing part-time in the negro church choir. Our church had two worship services, so it was easy for me to visit the African-American church and still attend my own congregation. And a few years later, my wife and I became members of the Board of Directors of Northcott Neighborhood House, just about four years after it was formed, and while it was in the process of trying to find its role in the African-American community in Milwaukee. We worked closely there, got well acquainted with many people, and one woman in particular became a close friend. She invited my wife and me to her home one week for Sunday dinner. And after dinner neighbors and friends came in and we had a delightful conversation. It wasn't until about 11:00, when the group broke up and we were getting in the car to go home, that I became conscious of the fact that my wife and I had been the only white people present.

"That's how much my prejudice had changed ... how nearly the racial bias had dissipated. I know in my heart that there's still a little of what I grew up with inside me, but I thank God that I've come so far toward getting over it."

Author's note:
This is a true story printed by the permission of Larry Wasson, a former member of Wauwatosa Avenue United Methodist Church, who currently belongs to First United Methodist Church in West Allis, Wisconsin. Larry told this story at a retreat on storytelling which John led for the West Allis church in 1995.

Trinity Sunday
John 3:1-17

Love In Action

"For God so loved the world that he gave his only Son, so that everyone who believes in him may not perish but may have eternal life."

— verse 16

Long ago, in the time before time, God was alone. It was not the nature of God to be alone, so God began to think. And as God thought, his thoughts became love and began to race across the void. His thoughts exploded across the emptiness and began to take the form of stars, galaxies, planets, suns and moons, and solar systems. God thought even more, and his thoughts became deeper and closer to his heart, and there came the earth and living things. And God loved it.

But God still felt alone. Suddenly God had a brilliant thought greater than all his other thoughts. Thus, in a great burst of love, God created human beings, male and female. God created them so that they could love him. It seemed so simple, so perfect. When God saw what he had done, a tear of joy came to his eye. God was no longer alone.

So perfect was God's creation, it was a shade of himself. He created people to be like him, so that they would think and create acts of love and caring. And God let them do that, and he stood back to watch. God was proud of what he had thought.

But there was a cost to be paid if love was to be perfect. And one day it happened. Although they did not say it in so many words, the humans God created and loved made it clear that they didn't love and need God anymore. God was concerned, but not terribly alarmed. God watched as his people tried to be like him. They really thought that they could be god themselves. God was no longer happy, and began to feel alone.

God watched as the people thought and acted like him. Sometimes the thoughts would create love and caring, but, more often than not, the thoughts would create the opposite — greed, hatred, envy, jealousy, gluttony and waste. God watched as humanity's thoughts created not love, but war, pollution, injustice and a lot of death.

As God watched, he felt pain and loneliness. At times, God would become very angry because his creation would not love him. God became frustrated that something so simple and perfect had become such a mess. God felt alone, but it was not the nature of God to be alone, so God began to think.

God thought, if only he were human, he could sit down and talk to his people. If only he could meet them face to face, they would understand, and their thoughts would again create love, peace, and harmony, which were the very heart of God. But, God thought, I must go all the way. I must be one of them; be born, feel like they feel, join them in their pain and show them a better way.

So, God thought, and his thought became love, and he was born a human being. God was God, but also human. It was confusing, but if love was to be perfect, a price must be paid. There was much of his creation that was very good. Many times, God did not feel alone. He had friends who loved him, who traveled with him and listened to him. But some were offended by him. Some were shocked. Some were amazed, and some were angry. "You can't be God," they said. "Only God can do the things you do, like forgiving sins and freeing people to love and care." The idea was too dangerous, so they decided that it would be best if God died. God experienced pain and rejection and death. God was alone. But it was not God's nature to be alone, so God began to think, and his thoughts turned to love. His love swallowed up the death that surrounded him, and God, who was life itself, began to live.

There was no longer anything that could separate God from his people. A bridge of love now linked them. Those who saw God as a human being after he became alive loved him. God no longer felt alone. And to make sure no one would forget that God was God, he gave a bit of himself to each one who loved him. Every time the story of God and his love was shared among them, that piece of

God would grow. As it grew, people began to think like God. As they thought, their thoughts turned to love and caring.

Therefore, God looked down at his creation and rejoiced that many loved him. His thoughts turned to love, and that love, his Spirit, rested upon his people. Wherever his people went, with God's Spirit upon them, their thoughts would turn to love and caring.

So, as people shared their love for God, the Spirit brought the very precious essence of God himself. The people began to call that essence faith. As faith grew, more people said, "I believe in God," and "I love God," and their thoughts became loving and caring. As these people told the story of God's love to others who didn't understand, the Spirit brought them faith, God's love in action. And God smiled and was happy, because God was not alone.

Author's Note:
Rolf Morck, the author of this story, is pastor of Bethlehem Lutheran Church, near Wausau, Wisconsin.

Proper 4
2 Corinthians 4:5-12

Memorial Day Preacher

But we have this treasure in clay jars, so that it may be made clear that this extraordinary power belongs to God and does not come from us. We are afflicted in every way, but not crushed; perplexed, but not driven to despair; persecuted, but not forsaken; struck down, but not destroyed; always carrying in the body the death of Jesus, so that the life of Jesus may also be made visible in our bodies. For while we live, we are always being given up to death for Jesus' sake, so that the life of Jesus may be made visible in our mortal flesh. So death is at work in us, but life in you.

— verses 7-12

I walked through the cemetery one evening, late in May. It was a way of preparing myself for the sermon I would deliver there at the Memorial Day service the following day.

The air was filled with the glorious scent of lilacs as I strolled among the graves. I marveled at the beautiful, full-grown maples and oaks, the lush green of the well-fertilized, close-cropped grass, and the loveliness of the flower beds bursting with red and white geraniums. I walked by many striking monuments, some from the Civil War era, some from World War I and World War II, Korea and Vietnam. I came upon a platform carved out of stone. In the center was a modest pulpit also carved from stone. I stood behind the pulpit and looked out over hundreds of graves: a congregation of the dead. It was the quietest, most attentive congregation I had ever stood before. But I didn't have anything to say to them. As I contemplated the magnitude of their sacrifices, and those of their families and friends, I was filled with a woeful sense of my own inadequacy. Memorial Day preacher, indeed!

When I returned home, I received a phone call from a friend who is a retired United Methodist pastor and a veteran of World War II. Kendall Anderson was a fighter pilot with the 39th Fighter Squadron in the South Pacific. His son Curt was killed in Vietnam in 1969.

I told Ken about my visit to the cemetery, my melancholy walk among the graves, and about standing in the pulpit at the war memorial, looking out on the congregation of the dead and not having anything to say to them.

Ken said, "Were you quiet enough to let them speak to you?"

Author's note:

Kendall Anderson is a retired United Methodist pastor who lives in Turtle Lake, Wisconsin.

Proper 5
Genesis 3:8-15

Becoming

... the Lord God called to the man, and said to him,
"Where are you?" He said, "I heard the sound of you in
the garden, and I was afraid, because I was naked; and
I hid myself." He said, "Who told you that you were
naked? ..."

— verses 9-11a

In the beginning, Adam and Eve were living happily ever after. They were the first human family. They were created in the image of God. God's name in those days was Elohim, which means "God." God told them to be fruitful and multiply. The human family was destined to grow and become.

Strange are the ways of Elohim, for Elohim is a God of adventure and imagination and curiosity. He created things not even being sure how they would turn out. They would just become. It was the holy genius of creation. Elohim simply thought and something popped out. It was wonderful! It was awesome! It was divinely unpredictable!

Elohim was so good at this "creating" that he decided to create something that was like him: something that would enjoy curiosity, adventure and spontaneity as much as he did. Well, out popped Adam and Eve, and they became a family.

Adam and Eve delighted in the world God had created. They went around discovering and adventuring. Elohim told them they could become anything they wanted. They could do anything they wanted, because God had placed in them his own imagination, creativity and sense of adventure. "To all of this," Elohim said, "there is just one condition. I am God, and you are not. The only limit you have is that; I am your God. Simple enough? It's not? Well, let me put it another way. You see that tree over there? That is the Tree of the Knowledge of Good and Evil. That is your limit.

That tree separates me from you. You can eat of any tree you want, except that one. If you eat of that one, you die. Deal? Okay."

To Adam and Eve it all seemed simple enough. And death didn't seem to be real, so why worry about it? Besides, with everything else in the garden, there was no need to bother with that one tree.

Adam and Eve got along splendidly. They enjoyed discovering and adventuring together, and they talked about their adventures with great delight. As they lived together and adventured together, they grew and became. And as they became, they rejoiced in being human, for to be human was never to stay the same. Each day was an adventure in creation. As they interacted with the world around them, the delights of creation amazed and transformed them. Adam and Eve grew up. They were responsible. They responded to the creation around them, and as they responded newness poured out of every corner. It was a delightful time to be a human family.

Then, one day, Elohim ran into Satan.

We don't know where Satan came from. That's the way stories are. They don't always explain, they just describe what is real. Now, Satan was a real devil. His job was to keep things from becoming. Satan believed in limits and keeping things the same. He didn't believe in becoming. Satan was the inventor of boredom.

So, Elohim ran into Satan one day, and Satan said, "Say, Elohim, nice creation you've got here. How do you keep up with it all? Nothing ever seems to be the same, and there's no way to predict what will happen next. Do you ever wonder if this spontaneous adventure thing might go too far? How will you know if your creatures become like you, which means they would have to put up with the likes of me! Take Adam and Eve over there. They are a lot like you. But then, they have limits, don't they? They know they are not God, don't they? I have to hand it to you, Adam and Eve are a real piece of work!

"But, Elohim, what if they *did* become like you? What would happen to them then?"

That made Elohim think. Putting limits on his creation was against his nature, for he was a God of becoming and possibility. All Elohim really wanted was for his creation to love him. In fact, that was so important to him that it meant he had to allow for the possibility that his human creation would NOT love him.

So, Elohim stated his position clearly to Satan. "I am Elohim, the God of becoming, curiosity, adventure and delight. I cannot compromise that, even if it means losing that which I love." And that was all that Elohim said.

That made Satan think. How can I trick humanity into doing something that is essentially against his or her nature? How can I get them willingly to choose limits: make them choose to be stuck and enable them to see life as boring? Suddenly Satan had a brainstorm.

"I've got it! I will limit them by simply offering them unlimited possibility! I will tempt them across the boundary that separates them from God and I will use the curiosity of the Creator to do it. A devilish plan, if I do say so myself!"

So, Satan waited patiently for the proper moment, until one day it happened. Eve was wandering near the Tree of the Knowledge of Good and Evil, oblivious to Satan's presence. Silently he moved close to her and plied her with a question that questioned God himself. "Did God say," he asked, "that you shall not eat from any tree in the garden?" Eve was startled by the question. Maybe God didn't have it right, after all!

So Eve stated that part of God's limitation that she most deeply believed. "We may not eat of the tree that is in the middle of the garden, or we will die."

"You won't die!" Satan said. "You will only have 'unlimited possibility.'"

So, Eve crossed the boundary between good and evil. And Adam as well. At that moment, life began to change. It became scary, because it contained both good and evil. Life became filled with fear, blame, shame and pain. It became an awful choice. One could choose not to risk, and keep things the same, denying what Elohim had created one to be; or one could choose to risk. Risking brought back the thrill of becoming, but because humanity now saw life with eyes that could see both good AND evil, they couldn't be certain how things would turn out. Fear led to limits, and limits led to sameness and boredom. Satan smiled. His plan was complete.

From generation to generation, this fear was passed on. Parents looked at children and, though they were filled with the love of Elohim, the creator God, for their children, they saw the risk involved in their "becoming." And they were afraid. Consequently, children learned to fear, like their parents. Life became filled with rules: tons of rules! Rules were intended to hide the fear. They were a safety net against failure. They also limited curiosity, adventure and becoming.

Rules began to rule on what one could become. So afraid did humans become that they willingly chose boredom and sameness. This boredom caused frustration because to stay the same and be bored was not the nature of humanity. Humans began to fight and blame each other. They couldn't figure out why they were so unhappy.

So humans left their families and started new families. New Adams met new Eves and fell in love. They hoped they could save one another from the boredom of life and the many rules. They simply sought to become.

But after a while they became afraid, because to risk in a world with good and evil in it meant the possibility of failure. And rather than risk, which could mean failure or the possibility of growth, they chose limits, rules and boredom. They began to fight and blame one another for their lack of happiness. They were no longer able to respond in creative and playful ways. They were no longer "response-able" to challenge, risk and newness. Relationships began to die. Families suffered.

Of course, this life was not at all what Elohim intended. Families were places where the spirit of adventure, creativity and curiosity were to be taught and nourished. So, over and over again, Elohim stated his position to his creation:

> *In my image you are to become. The only limit is that I am God and you are not. It is when you forget this that you end up on the dark side. For you seek from each other that which only I can give. You are not gods.*
>
> *Do not turn to your husband or wife, child, mother or father, and make them responsible for your happiness.*

That happiness, joy, curiosity, and sense of adventure which is life itself is my gift to you. Each of you is to use that gift for the benefit of the other, but you are not to seek that gift from one another. That is the limit of living with me, Elohim, the Lord your God.

Author's Note:

Rolf Morck, the author of this story, is pastor of Bethlehem Lutheran Church, near Wausau, Wisconsin.

The Mighty Acorn

He also said, "With what can we compare the kingdom of God, or what parable will we use for it? It is like a mustard seed, which, when sown upon the ground, is the smallest of all the seeds on earth; yet when it is sown it grows up and becomes the greatest of all shrubs, and puts forth large branches, so that the birds of the air can make nests in its shade."

— verses 30-32

A church camp counselor gathered the six small boys from his cabin under the spread of a very old oak tree. He instructed them to join hands around the gnarled trunk. By stretching with all of their might, and standing on their tiptoes, they were able to encircle the ancient tree.

"Look up now," the counselor called out to the campers. "See how many branches you can count." Each of the boys counted a different number of branches. There were more branches than any one boy could see from his perspective and the leaves were so thick that they could barely see the sun. One boy spotted a bird's nest near the top of one of the branches and three boys reported a squirrel scampering from limb to limb in an effort to escape from their view.

Then the counselor bid the boys to let go and join him in a circle under the tree. He instructed them to close their eyes as he picked up an acorn that had fallen from the tree. The counselor held the acorn up next to the trunk of the tree and then asked the boys to open their eyes. "This great oak was once a small acorn like this," the counselor said. "Now it is over a hundred fifty years old; it is two hundred feet high and has hundreds of branches. Birds, squirrels and many other small animals make their homes in its branches. God has made something that is very small grow into

130

something that is very, very large. If God can do this with a tree, consider what God is doing in your lives."

Then the counselor opened his Bible and read the parable of the mustard seed. When he was finished he asked the boys to lie on their backs on the ground and look up at the tree. As the boys looked upon the glory of the mighty oak that had grown from the small acorn, the counselor told them about the kingdom of God.

Out Of The Whirlwind

*Then the Lord answered Job out of the whirlwind: "Who
is this that darkens counsel by words without knowledge?
Gird up your loins like a man, I will question you, and
you shall declare to me."*

— verses 1-3

Frank Marshall had never felt so confused or helpless in his
entire life. He sat in his car, in his private parking space before the
corporate office of the company he had singlehandedly built. But
the sight of his professional domain failed to comfort him, as it
always had before. All that he had worked so hard for was crashing
down around him, and, for the first time in his life, he was at a loss
as to how to stop it.

Now, Frank had always had a thing about control. He knew
when he was in grade school what he wanted to do with his life.
By the time he was in college, majoring in business as he had
planned, he had decided exactly what type of girl he wanted for his
wife. He hadn't settled for anything less, pursuing the different
young women he met until he found just the one he was looking
for. Then young Frank had dated, wooed and won Marian, but
insisted on a long engagement so that he could finish college and
establish himself in business. In that way, he had provided her
with the home, income and lifestyle he had always envisioned.

To say that Frank Marshall was a perfectionist would be quite
an understatement. He prided himself on being in complete control
in his business, his finances, their church, and their personal life.
He not only planned each aspect of their lives carefully, he fully
expected the plans to be fulfilled within reasonable parameters of
his time frame. Marian had joked, when their two children were
born, that if the first hadn't been a son and the second a daughter,
as Frank had "ordered," she didn't like to think *what* would have

132

happened! She knew without a doubt, however, that he would *not* have succeeded in sending them back!

Frank loved his children, especially his son. He had always known that Andrew would grow up, go to college, and join him as a partner in his business. He had planned it that way. Christine, his daughter, he envisioned as a teacher. From the time she could talk, she had taken the roll of director, coordinating, leading and instructing her brother and friends in all of their activities. Frank had no doubt that she would be very successful.

It was Andrew about whom Frank had cause for worry. Although Frank had taken him to the office from the time he was three or four, teaching him little things, and, as time passed, bigger things about the business, Andrew showed little interest. He had a quick mind and a good grasp of the basics, but his heart was never in it. Frank quizzed him periodically on his interests, but they were constantly changing. When Andrew was twelve he wanted to play professional baseball. When he was sixteen he wanted to join the space program and studied hard in math and physics. After Andrew graduated from high school, he shocked everyone by announcing that he had decided to join the Marines. Fortunately, Frank had been able to block that whim, since Andrew wasn't yet eighteen. And so they had entered into four stormy years of college, which stretched into five and then six. Andrew continually changed majors until Frank despaired that he would ever actually graduate.

In the meantime, Christine graduated from high school and attacked college with a vengeance. Halfway through her first semester, she asked her father for permission to work part-time in his office. His daughter was so dedicated and efficient that Frank had no problem with allowing her to work for him. Letters arrived every semester from the University announcing that Christine had once again made the dean's list. She graduated *summa cum laude* the same year Andrew decided to drop out of college and join the Peace Corps. Her degree was in Business Administration.

Frank Marshall's perfect world crumbled that same spring when he learned, several weeks too late to act upon it, that Andrew was shipping out to Central America. His latest college courses in agriculture qualified him to be an advisor to the poor native farmers whose lands had been devastated by warfare and natural disasters.

Christine, determined girl that she was, proposed that she become her father's partner in the family business. That had always been her intent, from the time that she had been allowed to visit her father's office with Andrew and sit in his big leather chair behind his polished mahogany desk. Frank, however, had not planned for this. It was not Christine he wanted as a business partner. She did not fit into his vision for the future. He had meant for her to be a teacher, not a partner. That was still Andrew's place.

Angered by her father's unfairness, but ever practical, Christine applied for a position with his most fierce competitor. Her talent, drive and cunning moved her up quickly through the company ranks, and it was soon *her* plans and projects that caused her father serious business grief.

Frank Marshall was devastated. A lifetime of plans, his business and his family life fell apart before his eyes, and he became despondent. Marian tried to comfort him, but she could not fully understand the depth of his pain. After all, both of their children were happy and fulfilled in their work. She had tried explaining to Frank that there was a time to let go of one's children and let them live their own lives. Marian thought he should rejoice that they were successful and happy. She graciously refrained from saying that it was Frank's own fault. But Christine, truly her father's daughter, was not so kind.

"Just where do you get off, Daddy, thinking that you can run everyone and everything your own way? Who died and made you god, anyway?"

And so, Frank Marshall sat in his car, in his private parking space before the corporate office of the company he had singlehandedly built, and pouted. Where had things gone wrong? He had planned it all so carefully. How could God let this happen to him?

Proper 8
Psalm 30

If I Live To Be A Hundred

*Sing praises to the Lord, O you his faithful ones, and give
thanks to his holy name. For his anger is but for a moment;
his favor is for a lifetime. Weeping may linger for the
night, but joy comes with the morning.*

— verses 4-5

Sam Duncan lay in the semi-darkness of his nursing home room
performing the only two activities of which he still considered
himself capable: watching and waiting. Although his eyesight was
dim, he could still make out the steady brightening of the light of
dawn through the window next to his bed. And although his hearing
was too far gone to catch the rumble of the medicine cart, as it
worked its way up the hall toward his room, he could sense that the
time for his morning pills was near. He waited for the nurse to push
open the door and greet him and his roommate Arthur, who was
still snoring loudly in the bed next to his.

Most of the accepted measures of quality of human existence
no longer affected Sam. While time, in terms of years, seemed to
slip away unnoticed, the hours of the day crept by in agonizing
slowness. Time no longer meant anything to him. Schedules all
belonged to the nurses and aides and family members who waited
on him. He himself had no claim to time. The staff dieticians and
cooks decided what he would eat, and when. The aides assigned to
care for him on any given day decided when he would be bathed,
dressed, shaved, and even toileted. His family decided what clothes
he needed, what treats to bring to him, and when he should go out.
The activity director decided when he needed exercise, stimulation
and entertainment, and he was delivered into her hands by the aides
upon request.

There were few days when Sam could tell you what had occurred
the day before, or even the hour before. He had little memory for

what he had eaten for dinner Tuesday or breakfast Saturday. He seldom knew the day of the week or the correct month, although seasons were still instinctively evident. The minutia of every day had ceased to have meaning for him even before his nursing home days had begun ten years earlier, and he felt no concern or remorse over loss of interest in such trivia. But if you asked him if he remembered Pearl Harbor, or the day Franklin Roosevelt died, or what he was doing the day JFK was assassinated, he could tell you with detailed clarity what had gone on. He recalled vividly his wedding day, the day he and Martha buried their firstborn infant son, the details of the funeral of his grandson Sam who was killed in Vietnam, and what the weather was like on the day Martha died.

Sam also remembered the friends who had been most dear to him. They had all been gone for many years: Boots Martin, who had served with him in Germany in WW I; Alvy Hankins, who had gone to school with him and farmed outside of town; Dick Travis, who had been his business partner for nearly forty years ... all dead and buried long ago. It hadn't seemed unnatural that he had outlived them all, just part of life. But when he had outlived all of his children, the burden of life had become heavy, cumbersome. And now, at 102, it was nearly unbearable.

Sam had never been a complainer. Life was what it was. He didn't second-guess nature or the Creator. When he and Martha lost that first baby son, they had grieved and comforted one another, and eventually gone on with their lives. And God had blessed them with six healthy children who had survived well into old age. The death and destruction he had seen in the trenches during "the war to end all wars" was etched in his memory for all time, and yet he had survived it, both physically and emotionally. But when his grandson, young Samuel Wilks Duncan III, had been killed in Vietnam at the tender age of nineteen, it had taken much prayer and effort to overcome his sense of anger and grief. And when Martha died in 1989, at the ripe old age of ninety, and his own heart beat on strong and steady, even though he knew it was broken, he had shaken a mental fist at God and demanded to know why. Why must he be left to bear the burdens of life alone? At 93, why couldn't he go home, too?

136

That had been ten years ago. Ten years of slowly declining health, gradual loss of sight, hearing, movement and body function. Ten years of being taken here and there, regardless of his own wishes, by those whose job it was to provide him with comfort, stimulation, and quality of life. His grandchildren became so busy with their own lives that they seldom visited. And when his last surviving daughter had died of cancer last year at the age of 75, Sam couldn't help but wonder if God was allowing him to be put to the test, as he did Job. He felt very keenly the truth of Jesus' words in the Gospel of John:

> ... when you were younger, you used to fasten your own belt and go wherever you wished. But when you grow old, you will stretch out your hands, and someone else will fasten a belt around you and take you where you do not wish to go.

And so Sam had formed a mental list of Psalms from which to pray in all of his various moods:

> *How long, O Lord? Will you forget me forever? How long will you hide your face from me? How long must I bear pain in my soul, and have sorrow in my heart all day long?* — Psalm 13:1-2

> *My God, my God, why have you forsaken me? Why are you so far from helping me, from the words of my groaning? Oh my God, I cry by day, but you do not answer; and by night, but find no rest.* — Psalm 22:1-2

> *Even though I walk through the valley of the shadow of death, I fear no evil; for you are with me; your rod and your staff— they comfort me.* — Psalm 23:4

> *As a deer longs for flowing streams, so my soul longs for you, O God.* — Psalm 42:1

> *Do not cast me off in the time of old age; do not forsake me when my strength is spent. For my enemies speak concerning me, and those who watch for my life consult together.* — Psalm 71:9-10

*Sing praises to the Lord, O you his faithful ones, and give
thanks to his holy name. For his anger is but for a moment;
his favor is for a lifetime. Weeping may linger for the night,
but joy comes with the morning.*   — Psalm 30:4-5

Joy comes with the morning ... Sam's litany came to an end as the
nurse pushed through the door with the medications.

"Good morning, Sam. Wake up, Arthur! It's time for your
pills. It's a special day, Sam. Do you remember what day it is?"

"I don't know. Tuesday, maybe?"

"No, Saturday. You're going to have a lot of company today. This
is your birthday, Sam. Do you remember how old you are today."

"I guess I'd be about 103."

"That's right. One hundred and three years old. Everyone is
coming for your birthday party today. All of your grandchildren
and great-grandchildren, and I've heard you even have a couple of
great-great grandsons."

"I think they even named one of them after me."

"Well, April will be in in another hour or so to give you your
breakfast and bath. When you're all dressed and ready, we'll take
some pictures with all of your friends. Happy Birthday, Sam!"

One hundred and three. As he swallowed his pills, Sam's mind
drifted back to the lighthearted days of his youth, when he and his
friends used to say things like, "I'll never understand that if I live
to be a hundred." Things don't really change, Sam thought. I've
lived to be more than a hundred, and there are so many things I still
don't understand. "Do not cast me off in the time of old age."
"Weeping may linger with the night, but joy comes in the morning."
Sam sighed and laid back to watch and wait.

Author's Note:

This story first appeared in *Life Stories: A Study in Christian
Decision Making* by John Sumwalt and Jo Perry-Sumwalt, CSS
Publishing Company, Inc., Lima, Ohio, 1995.

Proper 9
Mark 6:1-13

A Prophet Without Honor

"Is not this the carpenter, the son of Mary and brother of James and Joses and Judas and Simon, and are not his sisters here with us?" And they took offense at him. Then Jesus said to them, "Prophets are not without honor, except in their hometown, and among their own kin, and in their own house."

— verses 3-4

There was once a young man who grew up in a small farming community. His father was of the third generation to plow, plant and harvest the family farm. He milked 40 head of cows, raised pigs and sheep, and tended 150 acres of land with the help of his four sons.

The young man loved the land. He spent his childhood wandering its hills and valleys, swimming and fishing in its creeks, picking its wild nuts, berries and fruits, and learning from his father all of the techniques of farming that had been passed down and learned and improved upon by three generations. And, when he was old enough, Josh Watson decided to go away to college to study agriculture and learn even more ways to improve the family farm.

Josh's father was proud that his son would follow in his footsteps, and those of his grandfather and great-grandfather. His greatest desire in life was to have their family farm continue to be passed down from generation to generation. He went on farming with his three younger sons until the eldest, newly graduated from the University, came home at last to rejoin them.

It was only a matter of weeks after the young man's return, however, before trouble began to erupt. Josh began to share his newly acquired knowledge and ideas and bombard his father and brothers with plans on how to accomplish the farmwork more efficiently, more productively, and more safely. Not only did he openly criticize some of his father's methods, but began to lecture neighbors and friends as well. Contour plowing, eliminating the use of DDT, stopping run-off of manure and pesticides into creeks and rivers: each thing he suggested opened a new wound. A mid-morning coffee break at the cafe in town, or a conversation over the corn grinder at the feedmill, often resulted in harsh words and bruised egos.

"Who does he think he is, anyway?" the neighbors asked.

"Yeah, old Ben Watson would turn over in his grave if he could hear the things that young'un wants to do to 'his' farm."

"The kid's still wet behind the ears. Let him try his new ideas and fall on his face. That'll teach him there's a difference between real farming and book learning."

And when his own father admitted that the young man's ideas were too radical for him, as well, Josh Watson became quite depressed and withdrawn. He began to consider his options, and within four months he left home to join the Peace Corps.

The young man traveled to strange, distant lands, where food, water and hope were scarce. He learned right away that attitudes everywhere were similar to those of his family, friends and neighbors. But the young man had regained faith in his own ideas. He believed that God had led him to those who needed his knowledge the most. Within four years his careful planning and implementation ended the famine. New sources of fresh water were located and wells dug. Irrigation systems were devised and put to use. New farm animals were introduced for food and to provide eggs, milk and cheese. Josh applied all of his training, and the farms began to sustain the people.

The folks at home continued to farm in their own familiar, comfortable ways. They read newspaper accounts of the young man's success, and his letters, and were thankful that he had found a place that "needed" his kind of learning, for they still believed that they did not. But the people whose lives were changed by Josh Watson's work praised him for his knowledge and skill. They admitted that they owed him their very lives, and thanked God for his presence among them.

140

Proper 10
Amos 7:7-15, Mark 6:14-29

Heads Will Roll

---

*Then Amaziah, the priest of Bethel, sent to King Jeroboam
of Israel, saying, "Amos has conspired against you in the
very center of the house of Israel; the land is not able to
bear all his words. For thus Amos has said, 'Jeroboam
shall die by the sword, and Israel must go into exile away
from his land.'" And Amaziah said to Amos, "O seer, go,
flee away to the land of Judah, earn your bread there and
prophesy there; but never again prophesy at Bethel, for it
is the king's sanctuary, and it is the temple of the kingdom."*

*Then Amos answered Amaziah, "I am no prophet, nor a
prophet's son; but I am a herdsman, and a dresser of
sycamore trees ...."*

— Amos 7:10-14

*Immediately the king sent a soldier of the guard with
orders to bring John's head. He went and beheaded him
in the prison, brought his head on a platter, and gave it to
the girl.*

— Mark 6:27-28a

Both management and union leaders were angry with Amos
Dresser. To management he was a whistleblower and to the union
he was a snitch. Amos had committed the unpardonable sin of
speaking the truth in a company where it was understood that certain
production practices were never to be questioned or mentioned.

Amos broke the unspoken and unwritten rule. He asked
questions of workers who became ill after coming into contact with
illegal materials that were used in the manufacturing process. And
when he discovered that the public was also endangered by the use
of these contraband substances, Amos made a speech at a public

141

meeting which was attended by members of the press. His charges about the company's use of illegal materials and the complicity of union leaders was front page news for several weeks. Amos appeared on three national talk shows and testified at a special legislative hearing at the state capitol. The company paid fines of several million dollars and the union president was defeated in the next election.

Still, the rank and file were generally displeased with Amos' public protestations. Some accused him of being a publicity seeker. Others said the company could have been held accountable without all the fuss of stories in the media. Amos reminded them that he was just a guy on the line who felt he had a duty to keep his co-workers and the public safe. "I want to do my job and be left alone," Amos said. But few believed him, and none of his co-workers called him friend.

When Amos' work was declared to be unacceptable in his next performance review, the supervisor insisted that the negative rating had nothing to do with Amos' public stand. And when Amos' section was down-sized and he was laid off without severance pay or pension benefits, no one spoke up to defend him. "That's what he gets for being a snitch," some of Amos' co-workers said behind his back. "That'll teach him to stick his neck out."

Proper 11
Ephesians 2:11-22

No Longer Strangers

So he came and proclaimed peace to you who were far off and peace to those who were near; for through him both of us have access in one Spirit to the Father. So then you are no longer strangers and aliens, but you are citizens with the saints and also members of the household of God ...."

— verses 17-19

Milenko and Eldina Sunjic came to the United States as refugees from Bosnia in July of 1994. Their son, Dorian, was just four years old, and their son Vedran was born one month later, after they moved into an apartment on West Wells Street in Milwaukee. In late October of that year, our church in Wauwatosa offered Milenko a job as custodian. He and his family moved into the old parsonage next to the church, and he began his duties during the first week in November.

In January of 1996, our Global Ministries Commission invited Milenko and Eldina to tell their stories at the Mission Festival. Over 125 people crowded into Youth Hall on January 21 to hear them speak. John kidded Milenko afterward that the custodian hadn't set up nearly enough chairs.

Everyone was impressed by Milenko and Eldina's excellent grasp of the English language after just eighteen months in the United States. And we were deeply moved by their stories. Twelve years ago, when she was fifteen, Eldina was one of the dancers in the opening ceremonies of the 1984 Olympic winter games in the beautiful city of Sarajevo. Now much of Sarajevo lies in ruins, and she and Milenko find themselves far away from their beloved homeland. This is their story.

Eldina's Story

"Hello, Ladies and Gentlemen," the pretty, young blond woman said in a soft, heavily accented voice. "I am going to speak about my perspective of the war as a woman and a mother. First of all, I will tell you a little about myself before the war. I grew up just like most children in the world. I didn't care what nationality or religion other people were. I had friends of all different nationalities: Serbians, Croatians, Bosnian Muslims. We were very good friends. I danced with a popular folk dancing group. We performed all over Europe and I was very happy during that time.

"When I met Milenko, I heard for the first time in my life about people having hard times and problems because of their nationality. Milenko's family is Croatian/Catholic and had a very hard life. His two uncles left the country because of communism — and because of that the whole Sunjic family had to pay! They couldn't get a larger apartment. They lived in a little two-bedroom apartment — six of them. Milenko's father couldn't earn better pay even though he worked very hard. Milenko talked to me about other people in the same situation, and I was surprised! In my family, no one talked about politics and communism, so I didn't know about it. I just remember about one uncle who was in jail for six months because he used one wrong word. He was a journalist and in one short story he used a word that the communists didn't like, so after that my family was afraid to talk to me about communism. My family is Muslim.

"Later, when Milenko and I got married, we had a nice apartment. We bought all new furniture, a car and everything we needed for a good life. Milenko had a good paying job as a warehouse manager. I had my own beauty shop, so we had enough money, a good life, and soon, a beautiful, healthy son. We had no idea our happiness would last for such a short time. The war was beginning.

"At first, I was surprised. I couldn't believe people were fighting over land and domination! That was history that I learned about in school. But I did not have a lot of time to be shocked. Being a mother and mother-to-be during a war is so hard. Our son was past his second birthday, and babies that age can tell your feelings and

144

emotions just by watching your facial expressions. So, even though I was scared, I kept smiling and held him so he wouldn't feel my fear. That was hard to do, but I knew I had to be strong and protect my baby.

"We could hear grenades and shelling around us. Roads were closed and grocery stores were empty. Everybody was afraid to stay because of the food shortage. Milenko found a way to send Dorian and me to Croatia. There was only one way, and that was a dangerous trip over the mountains. In peacetime, a trip to Croatia would take around five hours, but over the mountains, with Serbian soldiers all around, it took fourteen! We didn't have food, milk, or water for our children. We were very hungry. We cried and felt helpless.

"However, we finally came to Croatia and the Red Cross settled us on an island called Brac, in a refugee camp. There we got food and a room, so we were safe. There were a lot of mothers with children in the same situation I was in. I heard a lot of sad stories. Every day someone came with bad news about someone's husband or father being killed, or someone who lost a whole family. I was nervous, waiting to hear bad news. This was a very hard time for me. During the day I was a good mother so my son didn't know that I was worried, but at night, when he was sleeping, I would cry! I didn't have contact with Milenko for a long time because the telephone line was dead. Finally, he was able to get through to me on the satellite military phone to let me know he was alive. I don't know which is harder, to be a refugee, helpless and worrying, or to be in the war in a dangerous situation, but together. We were refugees, separated from Milenko for more than two years.

"Finally, Milenko came to Croatia to live, with no injuries. I was happy we were together again. I learned that my family was alive and still in Bosnia. It was hard to hear we lost everything — our home, money, car, business, even our photographs — it was like we lost our past. But I felt those were things that we could have again, and, most importantly, we were alive and together. We were lucky. A lot of people lost their whole family; women were raped; men lost an arm or a leg. A lot of people are still separated from the people they love.

"Now we are here in this beautiful country, starting a new life. I hope we are past the hardest part of our life, and I am thankful to God for a chance for a new life. I am glad you are interested in learning about our tragedy and the tragedy in our homeland. Thank you."

Milenko's Story

Milenko, dark-haired, tall and strong, looked uncomfortable before the microphone. His voice was deep, but soft, more heavily accented and less certain than his wife's.

"Ladies and Gentlemen, dear friends! Before I begin my speech, I wish to greet you and thank you for your interest in the situation in our country. It is difficult to explain the total situation, but I will try to make things clear.

"Before the beginning of the war, we lived in a small city in central Bosnia, in the country called Yugoslavia. Originally, Yugoslavia was the Kingdom of Serbia, Croatia and Slovenia, but it changed after the first World War. The Kingdom of Yugoslavia, which remained the country's name until the second World War, means Kingdom of South Slavish. After World War II, a second Yugoslavia was created from parts of six republics: Serbia, Croatia, Montenegro, Macedonia, Slovenia, and Bosnia/Herzegovina.

"The collapse of communism in the Soviet Union and the change to a democratic form of government allowed the first free elections in Yugoslavia. New political parties won that first free election, causing changes inside Yugoslavia that were opposed to the wishes of Serbia and Montenegro. These Serb countries wanted to retain the old communist system. The Serbian army carried out attacks, first on Slovenia and Croatia, then on Bosnia and Herzegovina. The war in Bosnia and Herzegovina was terrible mostly because there is such a mixed population there, moreso than in any other republic. The first strike was deadly because the Serbians had a strong, well-organized army. Our republics were mostly unarmed, with no heavy weapons. Because of that, in the first few months the Serbian army took seventy percent of the Bosnian and Herzegovinian territory. I want to remind you that before the beginning of the war, Serbian people made up 33 percent of the population of Bosnia and Herzegovina, Muslims made up 44 percent, and Croatians made up seventeen percent.

"Many areas of our country were isolated by the fighting — even our own area in central Bosnia. People weren't prepared for war, and soon we were without food and other necessities for normal living. After the first attack, I was afraid for the safety of my family, and I decided to send them on a very dangerous trip to Croatia. I had to stay in our city because I was drafted into army duty. For a long time, I had heard nothing about my family — my parents, brother, sister, and their families. After a few months, I got a telephone call from my sister. She was in Croatia with her children, a refugee. She told me that our parents and our older brother's family were in northwest Croatia, also refugees. She didn't know anything about our older brother or her own husband. My youngest brother was with me, along with his wife and two daughters. During that time, it was difficult to see my brother's children live through the terrible situation we were in. They spent a few hours of every day in a shelter. There was shelling everywhere in our city. I had a hard time, being separated from my wife and son, but I was glad they were in a safe place, far from the war.

"The war affected many people. It was very serious and there was nothing anyone could do to change it. All people were very nervous, and demonstrated it in different ways. Some people were very distrustful and became aggressive. Others became frightened and looked for ways to stay alive. Worst of all was the feeling of helplessness.

"After the first few chaotic months, our people were successful in organizing and stopping the Serbian army's advance. During that time, I found out that my older brother was in southern Herzegovina. He and others from his town had been forced into the nearby mountains. After a few days, I succeeded in finding him, and our brother-in-law and a few cousins. While I was there with them, thousands and thousands of refugees began to enter my city, and other cities and towns of central Bosnia, daily from northern Bosnia. Soon there were about 10,000 refugees in my city, which caused a shortage of food. Distrust grew between local residents and the refugees, especially between the Croatian and Bosnian people. I expected to hear any day that a new war had broken out — for the arguments to become actual fighting. My youngest brother remained there, in isolation, with his family. I couldn't get back into our city because it was isolated by the war.

"During that time, Croatians, who were in the minority in Bosnia, retreated into Serbian territory. The Serbian army took men prisoners, but sent women and children back into Croatia. We were worried about my younger brother. We hadn't heard anything about him for a few days. Through the Red Cross, we found out that he was in a concentration camp, Manjica, in northern Bosnia. We were told by the Red Cross that they were making negotiations for the exchange of prisoners. After a few days, we received a telephone call from a friend saying my brother was alive and free. Although he was returned to an isolated area in central Bosnia, Kiseljak, we were glad that he was alive.

"I was finally able to travel to Croatia to find my wife and son, and our family was together again. I was very frustrated with the situation in Bosnia and decided to stay in Croatia to find a job and live with my family. But I couldn't find a job because there was still fighting in Croatia, too. We began thinking about leaving Croatia and going to a western country. We found an American organization for the naturalization of refugees in the U.S. I have two uncles in the U.S., so I was able to get an affidavit of relationship and soon we were here.

"After three months of living in Milwaukee, I was lucky to find a job in this church, and I am thankful to the people here who helped give me a chance for a new life. My family experienced tragedy, but there were a lot of other families who lost everything, so their tragedy was worse than ours.

"I am hopeful that our country will come to a peace agreement through the support of the U.S. and our country will finally have peace. I hope that people there will find a way to forgive one another. There are a lot of problems. They must find a way to rebuild destroyed factories, homes, schools, for a better future for them and their children. We are thankful for the U.S. government's support in negotiations and feel we couldn't reach a peace agreement without that support.

148

"We are able to have contact with other refugees here by telephone and letter. Recently, I found the telephone number of the best man from our wedding. He went to Belgrade before the beginning of the war. Right now he is in Sweden with his mother and daughter. He was very happy to get my call. Sometimes we receive letters from our friends in Bosnia, but not often enough, because the mail there isn't very efficient.

"Dear friends, my story is short, but I hope you can better understand the situation in our country. Thank you very much!"

Proper 12
John 6:1-21

The Feeding Of The Fifty

Jesus said ... "Where are we to buy bread for these people to eat?" ... Andrew, Simon Peter's brother, said to him, "There is a boy here who has five barley loaves and two fish. But what are they among so many people?" ... Then Jesus took the loaves, and when he had given thanks, he distributed them to those who were seated; so also the fish, as much as they wanted.

— verses 5b, 8b-9, 11

Nancy Baker's cooking had become something of a legend at Our Savior's Church. Whenever there was need for advice or action on a church dinner, Nancy's phone would ring, and she was nearly always happy to comply because she loved to plan and cook meals. In part, people's high regard for her expertise came from the fact that Nancy had taught Home Ecomonics at the local high school for thirty years. Equally important was their firsthand knowledge that her home-cooked meals were delicious. But the most likely reason Nancy was so often consulted was the miracle she had performed. Now, Nancy pooh-poohed the suggestion that there was any miracle involved, and her husband, Vince, jokingly referred to it as "The Feeding of the Fifty," but those who were present to assist did not take what she had done lightly. In their eyes, it had been a true miracle.

It had all come about because Our Savior's hosted an annual Leadership Training event for their denomination's area churches. A planning committee arranged for workshops in a variety of different leadership areas: trustees, parish boards, music, church school, finance and so on. Our Savior's provided meeting and worship space, music and snacks.

On the day of that most memorable of training events, the morning had dawned overcast and forbidding. Thunderstorms were forecast for the entire day. However, the church volunteers and workshop leaders arrived early and made their preparations. By 11:00 A.M., an hour and a half before showtime, the rain which had been falling all morning began to freeze. But salting and sanding trucks were out on the streets and highways, so the planning committee reasoned that, while the numbers of those in attendance might suffer, it was already too late to cancel the event.

Two hundred and fifty hearty souls had arrived at the church by 12:30, through an unseasonably late shower of heavy, wet snowflakes. The weather people on local radio and television stations were chuckling over this April snowshower, explaining that it was an Arctic blast that had veered much farther south than expected. Enjoy! they said. Christmas in April could be fun!

But, while the Leadership Training workshops kept their participants occupied, area businesses, schools and offices began to close. Snowplows made repeated passes along major thoroughfares, but the snow was relentless. Workshop participants who had come from a distance began to slip out a few at a time. By the 3:00 P.M. breaktime, several had returned saying it was no use — they couldn't get home in the raging storm conditions.

Pastor Erickson and the planning committee called the remaining 109 participants together in the sanctuary at 3:15.

"We have begun calling our nearby church members and constituents to find overnight accommodations for everyone who is stranded here," Pastor Erickson announced. "As soon as the phoning is completed, you can take turns contacting your families to let them know you are taken care of."

But the phoning netted only 56 available beds, couches, cots and rollaways within walking distance. When those people had been met and escorted away through the storm by their hosts, 53 stranded participants still remained.

"I can take four of you," Pastor Erickson announced, suggesting as diplomatically as possible that those with strong backs, muscles, and joints remain to sleep at the church, allowing four with more fragile constitutions to accompany him. The group graciously complied. But, as the telephone volunteers were being instructed on their next campaign for nearby blankets, pillows, sheets, and sleeping bags, someone brought up the problem of food.

"What will we feed those who are left here?"

City traffic was almost literally at a standstill. There were numerous cars abandoned as much off the streets as possible, most where they had become stuck or struck. Snowplows had been ordered back to the public works garages until there was a let-up in the storm, but still snow flew and blew with raging ferocity. The entire city had shut down, including any grocery stores or restaurants within walking distance. Two people whose car was stuck in a drift up the street had seen the lights on in the church and come in asking for shelter: 51 snowbound guests, four church volunteers, and no food.

"Have the phone volunteers ask for whatever food people can spare along with the bedding," Nancy Baker said sensibly. "God will provide."

And so, the nearby parishioners trudged out into the vicious storm one more time to deliver whatever they had to offer. And while the sparse volunteer crew helped their stranded guests find the most comfortable spots in the building for making up beds, or set tables for 56, Nancy Baker shut herself in the church kitchen with the hodgepodge of food offerings. There wasn't a lot to work with — mostly canned goods, a little hamburger and chicken, cheese, pasta, eggs and milk — but she began to rummage about the kitchen and work her magic.

The guests occupied themselves with get-acquainted conversations, and cards and board games from the youth room, after the eating and sleeping arrangements were completed. At 5:45 they were called to the tables by the clinking of a spoon on a glass by Nancy.

"Please, find a seat and let's pray before we eat," the pastor, who hadn't been able to make himself stay away, said as the group assembled and grew quiet. "Thank you, dear God, for the warmth and shelter of our church building, for the generosity of those who have provided food and bedding, and for the love and fellowship around these tables. Bless this food we are about to eat. In Jesus' name. Amen."

And then the kitchen doors opened, releasing wonderful aromas, and the four volunteers began carrying out bowls and platters and

152

casserole dishes full of steaming, mouthwatering food. And everyone ate their fill, with plenty to spare.

The story of the quality and quantity of the food offered at that meal grew as it spread in the days and weeks following the storm. When the snowplows had done their work, and the shovelers and snowblowers had freed trapped vehicles, and everyone had returned home (after an equally amazing breakfast!), Nancy Baker was already on her way to being a legend in Our Savior's Church history.

"Such a lot of fuss!" Nancy told Vince. "All I did was use common sense and the food on hand." She chuckled, "I told them God would provide!"

Proper 13
John 6:24-35

The Bread Of Life

Jesus said to them, "I am the bread of life. Whoever comes to me will never be hungry, and whoever believes in me will never be thirsty."

— verse 35

When the INNS shelter program for the homeless started in Kenosha, I signed up for the training to be a volunteer. After I was trained, I was assigned a three-hour shift on a Sunday night at Lord of Life Lutheran Church, several blocks up the street from my own congregation. My shift was to be from 8:00 till 11:00 P.M. I helped to register the homeless persons as they arrived. Each person received a foam pad for a mattress, a small pillow, a sheet and a blanket. After they had received their gear, we took them into the fellowship hall where they were to sleep on the floor. There was a row of tables and chairs dividing the room. Men slept on one side and women and children on the other. No children registered that evening, but one young woman was in the late stages of pregnancy. Before my shift was through her labor pains had started and an ambulance had been called to take her to the hospital.

In all, about 25 persons came to the shelter on that cold November evening. Most of them were young men in their twenties and thirties. It was evident that they all knew each other, probably because they had sheltered together before on the street and in the churches after the INNS program began. A few of the men were quiet and kept to themselves, but several of them gathered around a large African-American man named Bill, who seemed to be a kind of leader in the group. They shared a warm camaraderie that was a joy to behold. They did not have homes and, in most cases, jobs, but they had each other, and they clearly enjoyed one another's company.

About ten o'clock, I went into the kitchen to make popcorn and to distribute snacks that had been provided by members of the churches participating in the program. Almost everyone came to get a cookie and a cup of coffee and then went back to the table where some of the men were engaged in a game of cards. Bill brought out an apple pie which he said he had purchased from among the day-old items at one of the bakeries. He cut the pie up and began to distribute pieces to all of his friends. I stood there watching hungrily, hoping he might offer me a piece, too. I felt guilty about my feelings, because I knew I would be going home in an hour and I could have anything I wanted to eat out of our family's well-stocked pantry.

I stood there looking on, envious of their fellowship as I wallowed in my suburban yuppie angst. Bill must have sensed my hunger, because just then he looked up and asked if I would like to have a piece of pie. I eagerly said yes, and quickly joined him and the others at the table. It felt very good to be included in their group. As I ate my pie and joined in the conversation, I became aware that we were sharing what our Lord Jesus called "the bread of life," and I knew I was in his presence.

Proper 14
John 6:35, 41-51

The Unknown Camper

---

*Jesus said to them, "I am the bread of life. Whoever comes
to me will never be hungry, and whoever believes in me
will never be thirsty."*

— verse 35

One summer at Lake Lucerne, in the Hillcrest area, there
appeared in every week-long elementary camp a small child who
came to be called the Unknown Camper. He was first seen on
Monday of the first week, near the Chipmunk Cabin, picking
raspberries on the edge of the woods. He had on a Lake Lucerne T-
shirt, shorts and an official camp cap. When the director first spotted
him, she called out to him and asked which cabin group he belonged
to. The child didn't answer and immediately disappeared into the
woods.

The following week, the lifeguard counted 61 campers during
a buddy check. There were only sixty names on his roster. The
lifeguard noticed that one of the campers didn't have a buddy. When
he approached him to ask about it, the camper ran off into the woods
and was seen no more that week.

The next week, one of the counselors reported being wakened
by a noise in the night. When he turned on his flashlight to check
on his campers, he couldn't believe his eyes. There was an extra
camper in the spare bed. The counselor didn't recognize the camper
and he was sound asleep. He thought he must be from another
cabin and decided to sort it out in the morning. But the next morning
the extra camper was gone, and all of the other counselors insisted
that their campers had been tucked safely in their beds throughout
the night.

It was during the Mission Camp, midway through the summer
season, while the staff was watching a video of the annual mission

parade, that they found the first concrete proof of the Unknown Camper's presence. One of the counselors said, "Who is that camper bringing up the rear of the procession?" They all looked, but no one recognized the little boy who was dressed like all of the other campers in a Lake Lucerne T-shirt and cap. One counselor said, "He sat at my table during crafts and no one seemed to know who he was. I thought he was from one of the other units and had stayed late to finish his craft project."

The identity of the Unknown Camper remained a mystery until the last week of camp. The director began to watch for the little boy every day. Then she saw him one evening, sitting inconspicuously on the end of a log at the evening campfire service. The director went up to him, sat down beside him on the log and put her hand on his arm so he couldn't run away, as he had done so many times before. She talked quietly with the Unknown Camper for a long time. He told her that he lived on a farm with his parents on the other side of the woods. His parents were good, hardworking people, but they didn't have time to take him to church, and they couldn't afford to send him to church camp. For years he had watched the kids in the camp from the edge of the woods. They appeared to be having so much fun that he longed to join them and share in their games and crafts. He said he especially enjoyed listening to the singing and the stories around the campfire. One day, he came upon a Lake Lucerne T-shirt and a cap left behind by one of the campers. He decided that, if he looked like the rest of the campers, perhaps he could join in some of the fun. He said he usually made his appearances at the beginning of the week, before the counselors had learned the names of all the campers.

The director walked with Jimmy through the woods to his parents' farm. She told him that if his parents were willing, she would arrange a scholarship for him so that he could attend church camp the next summer as a full participant. She also contacted the pastor of the neighboring church, and he found a family that was willing to give Jimmy a ride to Sunday School and worship every week.

The following summer, Jimmy reported to Hillcrest for Mission Camp dressed in his Lake Lucerne T-shirt and cap. That year, he led the procession in the mission parade and he took his turn leading songs and telling stories around the campfire. When the camp was over, Jimmy said it was the most exciting week of his life. He said he couldn't wait to come back the next year.

Author's note:

This story is dedicated to the campers and counselors of the July 1990 Mission Camp at Lake Lucerne, near Neshkoro, Wisconsin, where the story was created, with special thanks to Camp Manager, Joel Jarvis.

In an alternate version of the story, the mysterious camper turns out to be a chipmunk named Mike who has eaten so much camp food that he begins to look and dress like a camper. He eventually joins the camp staff, goes on to seminary and becomes a pastor in The Wisconsin Conference of the United Methodist Church.

Proper 15
Psalm 34:9-14, Ephesians 5:15-20

The Fear Of The Lord

Come, O children, listen to me; I will teach you the fear
of the Lord. Which of you desires life, and covets many
days to enjoy good? Keep your tongue from evil, and
your lips from speaking deceit. Depart from evil, and do
good; seek peace, and pursue it.

— Psalm 34:11-14

Do not get drunk with wine, for that is debauchery; but
be filled with the Spirit, as you sing psalms and hymns
and spiritual songs among yourselves, singing and making
melody to the Lord in your hearts ... .

— Ephesians 5:18-19

There was no warning. One moment, busy afternoon rush hour
crowds were bustling in and out of the subway terminal. Men and
women of various ages, carrying briefcases, shopping bags,
backpacks and young children, brushed determinedly past one
another on their way to and from countless locations. A group of
tourists with floral print shirts and cameras craned their necks to
take in the vaulted ceilings and marble pillars of the old 96th Street
terminal as they descended into its artificially lit atmosphere. Two
teachers herded twenty children, on a late spring field trip, up to
the street on the adjoining staircase. Three youths, dressed like
gang members, surreptitiously drew out spray paint cans, and two
stood watch while the third emblazoned the wall behind one of the
pillars with gang symbols and slogans. No one seemed to notice,
or if they did, chose not to acknowledge the vandalism. It was the
end of the day. Almost everyone just wanted to get home.

The next moment, the ground began to tremble, as if the switch on
a giant vibrating machine had been thrown. Surprise registered on
every face, and people struggled to keep their footing. Many failed.

In another moment, the trembling became violent shaking. Crumbling concrete began to fall. Sharp, jutting segments of tiled floor rose up, exposing earth, and worse, gaping chasms beneath. Water pipes and electrical circuitry were torn free, creating showers of water and intermittent sparks. Artificial lights went out, avalanches of dirt and masonry fell, and soon all natural light from the former entrances and exits of the terminal was blocked out.

While it seemed an interminable amount of time to those who endured it, the quaking actually lasted less than one minute. When it ceased abruptly, so did the screams of the crowds. People who could move began to free themselves from debris in the total darkness. Voices called out names in terrified uncertainty; some were answered, some were not. Then, the sounds of weeping and moaning could be heard. Someone flicked on a cigarette lighter, but was urged to put it out immediately; there was no way of knowing if gas pipes had been ruptured nearby.

A voice called out for a flashlight, if anyone had one, and two or three came on. Those who were uninjured began to move among the immobile. Handkerchiefs, scarves and torn clothing became bandages and tourniquets. In a few moments, emergency generators kicked in and cast an eerie, but welcomed, yellow/orange light over the devastation.

People used to being in charge began to direct those who wandered aimlessly. Everyone trapped within the cavern created by the quake was accounted for, freed from the rubble, if possible, and gathered together in the most open, secure section of ground. Volunteers cared for the injured and covered the dead. Names were exchanged. The injured and strickened were comforted.

It was a small, elderly woman with a soft halo of white hair who discovered the boys behind the pillar. One, half buried in rubble, was unconscious. Another, clearly in shock, with blood streaming down his face from a scalp wound, sat rocking next to his unconscious friend. The third, clearly terrified, had withdrawn from the two and drank repeatedly from a pint-sized bottle of liquor. As yet, the alcohol had not dulled the fear in his eyes.

"Let's move your friend out into the open, away from this loose rubble," the old woman said softly to the uninjured boy. "Then we can get some men to free your other friend."

"Mind your own business, Grandma," the boy said angrily, and continued to drink from the bottle.

The old woman sought help for the injured youths, then made rounds of the others who were hurt and frightened. As time passed, with nothing to occupy time but thinking of their plight, fear and tension grew.

"What are we going to do to get out of here?" someone finally demanded loudly. "We can't just sit here, trapped."

"Don't touch anything!" cried another. "You'll cause an avalanche!"

"What about aftershocks," said another. "If more concrete falls, we could all be crushed!"

"Have faith," the small, white-haired woman implored. "Pray for help to come soon. God will take care of us."

"Like he took care of them?" shouted an angry voice, indicating the covered bodies of the dead. "No thanks!"

"This space is too small for all of us," cried a claustrophobe. "Stop arguing! We'll run out of air!"

Authoritarian voices demanded calm and quiet, but fear was much stronger than reason. Several people appeared to be near total panic. The gang youth with the liquor bottle began to laugh uncontrollably amid the shouting and crying, adding to the chaos, until it seemed there was no hope of restoring order and calm.

Suddenly the ground began to tremble beneath them again. Low rumbling rose into another terrifying roar as the movement increased to a shaking. The angry, frightened and hysterical voices were muted in terror, but mercifully, the shaking subsided without becoming a full-blown quake. The aftershock. And after its shock began to wear off again, amid the coughing and brushing off of dirt and dust, a soft, quavering voice could be heard singing a familiar hymn. Searching eyes identified the elderly woman, kneeling between the unconscious gang youth and his unresponsive friend with the head wound, holding the hand of one and soothing the brow of the other as she sang. No one spoke; every ear was intent on the song.

Be not dismayed whate'er betide, God will
take care of you;
Beneath his wings of love abide, God will
take care of you.

Through days of toil when heart doth fail,
God will take care of you;
When dangers fierce your path assail, God
will take care of you.

No matter what may be the test, God will
take care of you;
Lean weary one upon his breast, God will
take care of you.

The uninjured youth stared at the half-empty liquor bottle in his hand for a few moments, then tossed it at one of the piles of rubble. Gradually, the words became louder and clearer, until everyone who was able either hummed or joined in the refrain:

God will take care of you, through every
day, o'er all the way;
he will take care of you, God will take care of you.

Hours later, rescue crews worked feverishly to free the trapped and injured from the earthquake's devastation. Amid pain-filled moans and anguished cries on the street level, the peaceful sound of singing greeted them as they began the careful excavation of the old 96th Street subway terminal. And as the crews lifted those survivors to safety, the puzzle of their serenity was answered when a small elderly woman, with a halo of white hair, paused as she reached the surface, deeply inhaled the fresh night air, and said, "Thank you, Lord, for sending your Holy Spirit to comfort us in the hour of our need." Then the rescue workers smiled at one another as the woman was helped to an ambulance, humming the tune of the familiar hymn as she went.

Civilla D. Martin, "God Will Take Care of You," *The United Methodist Hymnal* (Nashville: The United Methodist Publishing House, 1989), p. 130.

Proper 16
Ephesians 6:10-20

The Wiles Of The Devil

*Put on the whole armor of God, so that you may be able
to stand against the wiles of the devil. For our struggle is
not against enemies of blood and flesh, but against the
rulers, against the authorities, against the cosmic powers
of this present darkness, against the spiritual forces of
evil in the heavenly places. Therefore take up the whole
armor of God, so that you may be able to withstand on
that evil day, and having done everything, to stand firm.*
— verses 11-13

Sandy Wright felt betrayed. She sat at her desk staring at the
papers in her hands, but she didn't see them. Her mind was still reeling
from the reprimand she had just received from Ken Martin, her
supervisor. But worse than that, she knew that the source of the
mistaken information Ken had used to chastise her was Kelly Fox;
and she knew that there was absolutely nothing she could do about it.

It had been just over a year since Sandy had joined the design
team at InfoTec. She loved her work, and had proven herself good
at it. Kelly had signed on just two weeks after Sandy, and while
her work was good, it wasn't always on target. She tended to get
sloppy when the workload was heavy and to overlook some of the
mistakes she could have corrected. Eventually, Ken had teamed
Kelly with Sandy, in hopes that Sandy's attention to detail would
rub off on her. They had worked closely on several assignments
and gotten along well.

It bothered Sandy that Kelly sometimes talked about Ken and other
team members behind their backs. Kelly had a way of insinuating
things about others which raised questions about their character and
motives. While she never actually gossiped, in terms of spreading
rumors, her hints at people's possible personal faults was just as
damaging. It was a subtle undermining of respect and authority. Sandy's

164

response to these covert attacks was usually to make no comment. However, she noted that if she countered Kelly's ideas, Kelly almost always backed down. In the back of her mind, Sandy knew that, if Kelly talked about others in this way, she probably talked about her to others as well. But, because they got along well, she didn't dwell on the idea. She resolved to keep their relationship on a friendly, professional basis, and ignore Kelly's less appealing characteristics.

Still, Sandy's attention was frequently drawn to Kelly's most annoying tendencies. While Kelly expected respect from others, she often placed herself in a position to receive sympathy. Her father was very ill with emphysema. When Kelly was having a bad day, she would often affect a sad-eyed, wounded appearance. This invariably drew attention from co-workers, who inquired about her father. And, even if he was not the source of her current malaise, Kelly revelled in their concern and attention. Other days Kelly was the life of the office, her laughter wafting over the cubicles. On those days, Sandy had learned not to expect much of a work contribution from Kelly, because she was too busy socializing. Everyone who passed by Kelly's desk was engaged in some kind of congenial conversation, which always ended in another wave of Kelly's lilting laughter. Kelly used these opportunities for name-dropping, hinting about her expertise in an area, and kissing up to management. The hardest part for Sandy to take, however, was when Kelly turned right around and cast aspersions on the characters of those she had just found so entertaining.

Because it was so easy for her to see what Kelly was really like, Sandy assumed that everyone else did as well. She herself had found a way of maintaining a comfortable work relationship with her by overlooking her idiosyncracies, and so, she assumed, had everyone else. In a few instances, their circles of friendship overlapped, but for the most part, Sandy separated herself from Kelly in all but their closest work situations. It was not until it was too late that she understood that Kelly's "idiosyncracies" were, in fact, a dangerous evil.

Sandy took pride in her work. Even when the loads were heavy, she liked to think ahead and be prepared. There were plenty of tasks she would leave until the last minute, but planning, scheduling and detail were priorities. Part of Kelly's job was to coordinate assignments for the various work teams so that there was true "team work" with a minimum of headbutting. Because Sandy paid close attention to detail, she always scheduled her assignments with Kelly well in advance. That was why, when she was called into Ken's office for a meeting with him and another team leader, Sandy was totally unprepared for the anger and criticism directed at her.

"It's been brought to my attention that you haven't been following policy on scheduling," Ken said sternly when Sandy and Mike, the other team leader, had been seated.

"I'm sorry?" Sandy replied, stunned by Ken's authoritarian tone and baffled by his statement.

"He's talking about the way you took over my slot in the May leadership conference and replaced my progress report with your training program," Mike said, unable to keep the anger out of his voice.

"There must be some mistake," Sandy said, keeping her voice even. "I scheduled my program with Kelly."

"When I spoke with Kelly a month ago about the time slot for my progress report, she said there was no problem. Then, when the memo came out Tuesday with the time schedule for the conference, your program was listed in my time slot. When I checked with Kelly, she told me that you often go over her head and change schedules. I came to Ken because I've heard that complaint from other team leaders, too. I thought it was about time that you hear how angry some of us are that you do this."

"It is always my practice to schedule programs well in advance," Sandy insisted. "Perhaps Kelly ..."

"Kelly has told me," Ken interrupted, "that you have often blamed her for scheduling errors. I know that I teamed you with Kelly to help her focus her work, but that shouldn't give you the right to blame her if you make mistakes."

Sandy could see that she had been placed in a no-win situation. There was nothing she could say or do. The only option was to back down.

"If I made a mistake, I apologize," she said, struggling to keep emotion out of her voice. "If Mike scheduled his presentation first, then he should have the time slot. I'll just have to make other arrangements for my program."

Both Mike and Ken looked a little surprised at that, and the meeting ended with awkward thanks. Now Sandy sat at her desk, staring at papers she wasn't really seeing, and trying to deal with the flood of thoughts and emotions in her head.

How could she have been so naive? Why, when she knew how Kelly treated everyone else, should she have expected to escape that treatment herself? Kelly had set her up to take the fall for her own scheduling mistakes, just as Sandy knew she set up and manipulated others. Why hadn't she anticipated it? And how could she prove anything? There was no proof. She only knew, from her observations and experience, what Kelly was like. What if she was the only one who saw it? Kelly herself was only an annoyance, but her actions were evil. Where could Sandy go with that? And, since Kelly had cast doubt on Sandy's character as well, what good would it do? It would only appear to be another attack on Kelly.

But how could Sandy go on working with her, never knowing when or where the next attack would come? She would have to be very careful from now on. She would have to document every move. And she would have to keep her ears open to hear who else had been stung. Perhaps, in time, she could make a case, but for now she would stifle her anger and suffer the humiliation. "Dear God," Sandy prayed silently, "help me handle this mess. Help me keep control of my temper and be there for others. Don't let me be vindictive. Most of all, let Kelly see how much hurt she causes. Help her break away from doing evil things."

Author's Note:

In the introduction to his book, *Evil: A Historical and Theological Perspective*, Hans Schwarz asks two questions which are addressed by this text and story: "Why is life on earth characterized by the fact that humans make life miserable for each other?" and "Is there a force within and yet transcending humanity that functions, as it were, as a diabolos or as a 'distorter,' continually

167

detracting from the experience of the good in our lives and turning it instead into something negative?" (p. 3).

In *Antagonists in the Church: How to Identify and Deal with Destructive Conflict*, Kenneth Haugk describes persons who act out destructively in the church, the way Kelly does in the story. Haugk says: "The spiritual forces that stand in rebellion against God and God's claim on people lie behind (indeed, precipitate) the behavior of antagonistic individuals...When confronting an antagonist, it must be kept in mind that antagonists play into the hands of forces that are intent upon destroying the healing and caring missions of the church. One dare not sit back and watch antagonists cripple and disfigure a congregational body" (p. 42).

M. Scott Peck observes in *People of the Lie: The Hope for Healing Human Evil* that in his experience " ... evil human beings are quite common and usually appear quite ordinary to the superficial observer." He adds: "While evil people are to be feared, they are also to be pitied. Forever fleeing the light of self-exposure and the voice of their own conscience, they are the most frightened of human beings. They live their lives in sheer terror. They need not be consigned to any hell; they are already in it" (p. 67).

Peck believes that evil people cannot be "...rapidly influenced by any means other than raw power. They do not respond, at least in the short run, to either gentle kindness or any form of spiritual persuasion ..." (p. 68). "It is not their sins, per se, that characterize evil people, rather it is the subtlety and persistence and consistency of their sins. This is because the central defect of the evil is not the sin, but the refusal to acknowledge it" (p. 69).

Kenneth C. Haugk, *Antagonists in the Church: How to Identify and Deal with Destructive Conflict*, (Minneapolis: Augsburg Publishing House, 1988), p. 42.

M. Scott Peck, *People of the Lie: The Hope for Healing Human Evil*, (New York: Simon and Schuster, 1983), pp. 67-69.

Hans Schwarz, *Evil: A Historical and Theological Perspective*, (Minneapolis: Fortress Press, 1995), p. 3.

Proper 17
James 1:17-27

Unstained By The World

Religion that is pure and undefiled before God, the Father,
is this: to care for orphans and widows in their distress,
and to keep oneself unstained by the world.

— verse 27

So now, Israel, give heed to the statutes and ordinances
that I am teaching you to observe, so that you may live to
enter and occupy the land that the Lord, the God of your
ancestors, is giving you. You must neither add anything
to what I command you nor take anything away from it,
but keep the commandments of the Lord your God with
which I am charging you. You have seen for yourselves
what the Lord did with regard to the Baal of Peor — how
the Lord your God destroyed from among you everyone
who followed the Baal of Peor, while those of you who
held fast to the Lord your God are all alive today.

— Deuteronomy 4:1-4

A good friend of mine lives just two blocks from the Saint Croix Casino in Turtle Lake, Wisconsin. On a recent visit he offered to take my wife and me out for dinner at the casino restaurant. He said they had a wonderful Saturday night buffet and it was cheap. We readily accepted.

When we arrived at the casino I was struck by the size of the parking lot. There were acres and acres of cars. Our friend pointed to the spots where six houses had been torn down to make way for the parking lot. About one third of his neighborhood had been bought out by the casino. Where he used to look out on trees and houses with green lawns, he now sees pavement, lights, and security cameras. Recently the casino announced their intention to buy another block of houses, including our friend's house.

As we entered the casino I noticed the presence of numerous security officers. We paused for a moment in the large lobby area at the door, and after the guards had checked us through, we began to make our way slowly through the masses of people gathered around the slot machines. The flashing lights, the buzz of the machines as the levers were pulled, and the occasional sound of coins clinking in the slots were mesmerizing. Our friend pointed out that there are no windows and no clocks in the casino. All sense of ordinary time stops at the door.

When we finally made it to the dining area, which is located in the back of the casino, we were greeted by a friendly waitress who told us the Friday night buffet was just $8.75 and it was all-you-can-eat. Our friend was right; the food was wonderful. We had our choice of prime rib, fried chicken, roast beef, pork chops, deep fried scallops, baked ham, barbecued ribs, mashed potatos, gravy, a host of salads, vegetables, dinner rolls and all the trimmings.

The best part of the buffet was the dessert bar. There was a large selection of pies, cakes, puddings — and chocolate turtle cheesecake to die for. I had three helpings.

After the dinner we strolled out into the casino to watch the action. There was very little conversation. All eyes were on the slot machines and the blackjack tables. I especially enjoyed watching the blackjack dealers contend with what I imagined were veteran gamblers trying to beat the odds. From the little we were able to observe it seemed that the house almost always won. Sometimes one of the gamblers got lucky, but mostly they paid their money and, I suppose, counted it the cost of a night's entertainment.

Every once in awhile a teller would come out onto the floor followed by an armed guard. He would roll his cart up to the blackjack table and collect the money. The action would stop for a moment. The crowd became very quiet. All eyes were on the money and the armed guard. There was little doubt about what is considered holy and what is worshiped in that place.

On the way out we passed the sandwich stand where you can get a half-pound prime rib sandwich for $2.75. "Delicious," our friend said. "None better. No restaurant in town can compete with the quality or the prices of the food at the casino." We went into the gift shop and our friend showed us stack after stack of cigarette cartons. "Why so many cigarettes?" we asked. He pointed to a sign listing the price. A carton of Marlboros cost $17.94 at the casino. Across the street at the Holiday station the same carton sells for $21.01.

Few of the local merchants have been able to compete successfully with the casino. Many of the buildings on the main street of Turtle Lake are empty or dilapidated. Some of the remaining businesses are struggling. When the casino opened in 1992 there were high hopes that the increasing number of people coming to town would mean higher profits for local businesses. A million and a half people pass through the doors of the Saint Croix Casino every year, but very few of them shop at local businesses. People come by the busload from all over Wisconsin and the upper Midwest. A High Rollers bus ticket from Milwaukee costs just $45.00. Along with the bus ride you get a night's lodging at the Saint Croix Motel, a steak and lobster dinner in the casino restaurant, and a twenty-dollar rebate in chips to get you off to a good start on the slot machines. It is not known how many out-of-town guests patronize area prostitutes or drug dealers, the two local businesses which have seen an increase in trade in the past four years.

The Saint Croix Casino takes in an estimated 12 million dollars a month. Most of that money is not spent in the Turtle Lake community or anywhere else in Northwest Wisconsin. And because the casino is owned by the Saint Croix-Chippewa Indian Tribe, no money is paid in state, federal, or local taxes. The largest business in Barron County pays no school taxes, pays for no utilities, and pays for no fire department, police, or ambulance services. Most of the 1,000 employees at the casino get minimum wage and no benefits.

One young family man with a wife and three children, who works in the maintenance department at the casino, earns $4.95 an hour. He gets no health insurance and no pension. He could make $90.00 more per month if he quit his job and went on welfare.

Recently, a woman from a neighboring town was arrested for embezzling $450,000.00 from the business where she worked.

Much of the money was lost in gambling at the Saint Croix Casino. Unlike bartenders who will refuse to serve a perpetual drunk, the casino employees continued to take the woman's money until her life was ruined.

The next morning after our visit to the casino we went with our friend to worship at the local United Methodist church. The attractive new church building is located on a large lot on the east edge of town. The wood-paneled sanctuary is warm and intimate, about the same size as the lobby of the casino. The people were friendly and invited us to come again. I was especially moved by a children's choir that sang during the service. The quality of the music wasn't any better or any worse than the children's choir in my own church, but their smiling faces and the enthusiasm and the joy with which they sang about their love for Jesus touched my heart. At the same time I felt a deep sadness as I listened to their song. I knew many of these children would end up working at the casino when they were grown. I said a prayer for them under my breath: "O Lord, keep these beautiful children safe from the evil that is so powerful in this community."

Proper 18
Psalm 146

Keeping Watch

---

*Happy are those whose help is the God of Jacob, whose
hope is in the Lord their God, who made heaven and earth,
the sea, and all that is in them; who keeps faith forever;
who executes justice for the oppressed; who gives food to
the hungry ... The Lord watches over the strangers; he
upholds the orphan and the widow ....*

— verses 5-7, 9a

A little boy named Jacob was getting ready for bed. He had
brushed his teeth and washed his face; he had put on his favorite
red pajamas with a picture of a panda bear on the front; he had fed
his goldfish named Herbie and his hamster named Fred; he had
hugged all of the stuffed animals at the foot of the bed; his mom
had read him one of his favorite stories and now it was time to say
his prayers. He knelt down beside the bed, and was about to bow
his head and close his eyes, when he remembered to ask his mom a
question that he had been thinking about for a long time.

"Mom," Jacob said, "what does God do all day?"

"God watches over us," she replied.

"What does God do at night, when I'm asleep? Does God sleep,
too?"

"God is always watching over us, even at night while we are
sleeping," Jacob's mom said as she gave him a hug.

"God must get tired of watching sometimes," Jacob said. "I
wonder if God ever needs any help?"

Then he closed his eyes, bowed his head and prayed, "Dear
God, if you ever get tired and want to take a break, it's okay. I'll
help you watch."

Cross Foolishness

Then he began to teach them that the Son of Man must
undergo great suffering, and be rejected by the elders,
the chief priests, and the scribes, and be killed, and after
three days rise again. He said all this quite openly. And
Peter took him aside and began to rebuke him. But turning
and looking at his disciples, he rebuked Peter and said,
"Get behind me, Satan! For you are setting your mind
not on divine things, but on human things."

— verses 31-33

Emma stomped up the church steps and unlocked the front door. Her dinner appointment had kept her much later than she planned, and now she must hurry if she wanted to make it home on foot before dark. Walking home alone after dark was a serious concern, but it could not deter her from her family duty.

Keys still in hand, and without stopping to remove her coat, boots or scarf, Emma plodded to the storage closet near the secretary's office. She unlocked the door and turned on the light. There, in its place on the back shelf, encased in a handmade velvet cover, sat Grandfather Norman's cross. She removed the faded maroon cover respectfully, folded it and placed it on the shelf. Then she lifted the heavy, goldplated cross, which was very nearly as big as she, and gingerly backed out of the closet. She took extra care not to bump one of the crosspiece arms against the woodwork. Grandfather Norman had purchased this cross in the Holy Land in 1902, and had it shipped home at a great cost, as a gift to his church. After all these years it fell on her shoulders to see to its care and placement every week.

Not that there would be such a need if "certain circumstances" had not come about. Emma staggered a bit under the sheer magnitude of her burden as she made her way to the elevator. Once inside, she set the cross down on the carpeted floor and pressed the UP button. There was a slight shudder as the door closed and the compartment rose toward the sanctuary. If it weren't for "certain circumstances," and stubborn mules like Harvey Volkman, she wouldn't have been making these weekly rounds for the past 10 years.

Most of the younger members of the congregation knew nothing about "the circumstances." Most of the longtime members didn't care. But it was a matter of family honor for Emma, and a matter of pigheadedness, she could testify, on Harvey Volkman's part. Because Harvey had been the one who brought up the idea of the "old rugged cross" in the first place.

Fifteen years earlier, on March 12, 1980, Harvey Volkman had raised the idea of replacing Grandfather Norman's beautiful gold Holy Land cross with a rough-hewn, life-sized wooden cross. It would come complete with three metal spikes embedded where Christ's hands and feet would have been. To Emma's mother's horror, the Worship Taskforce had referred the idea to the Trustees, and the Trustees had actually brought it before the Church Council for discussion. Well, of course, Emma's mother had objected to such a ridiculous idea. She stated quite eloquently the importance of her father's loving and beautiful contribution to the worship experience of their church. And Harvey Volkman had had the gall to call Grandfather's cross a gaudy museum piece that had nothing to do with Jesus or his sacrifice for us.

Well, the battle raged back and forth, with members taking sides, until finally the Council chair had the presence of mind to table the discussion until a study could be done. Unfortunately, a mere five years later, their new pastor began a Saturday night service, and she bought Harvey Volkman's idea hook, line and sinker. The morning after that first Saturday night service, Emma and her mother entered the sanctuary early to find that "old rugged cross" still standing in the chancel. Grandfather Norman's cross had been unceremoniously dumped behind the altar, out of the way!

From that Sunday until her death, Emma's mother had carefully put the Holy Land cross away in the cover she made for it, in the locked closet, every Saturday morning. And she lovingly returned it to the altar after services every Saturday night. For the past 10 years, the duty had fallen on Emma.

She lifted the cross into her arms again. There was a strange pause when the elevator stopped, just before the doors slid open. And when they did, there stood Harvey Volkman, punching at the elevator buttons, with the "old rugged cross" perched on his shoulder just like Jesus on his way to Golgotha. When he saw Emma he snorted, kind of like an old bull. And instead of stepping aside to let her out, he barged right ahead, jamming that oversized woodworking reject right across the elevator door so Emma couldn't even pass. While he tried to heft it around so that it stood upright, he bumped the crosspiece arm into the button panel, which closed the door and started them down. Then, when he tried to turn to stop it, he bumped the buttons again, and the elevator jolted to a halt halfway between the floors.

Emma was fully prepared to tear into Harvey for his rudeness, until she saw the surprised look on his face and realized that he hadn't really meant to get them stuck. After a few minutes of his button punching, door pounding and calling for help, she set Grandfather's cross in the safety of the corner behind her. She helped lift the "old rugged cross" off Harvey's shoulder and lean it against the wall. Then she sat down as daintily as the limited space allowed. When another forty minutes had passed without any hope of rescue, Harvey Volkman did the same.

It was about 9:30 when Pastor Jones looked out her dining room window and noticed there were still lights on in the church. She had thought Harvey Volkman would turn them off when he put the cross away after the 5:00 service, as he always did. Running over to switch them off was no chore, and while she was there she remembered that she'd left her sermon notes on the pulpit. When she tried to take the elevator up to the sanctuary to get them, it didn't work, and she called the janitor.

Emma patted her hair and lifted Grandfather Norman's Holy Land cross into her arms when the elevator began to move again, after a lot of hammering and cussing by the janitor. She couldn't quite describe the looks on the pastor's and janitor's faces when the doors slid open to reveal her and Harvey, bearing their various crosses. Nor would she have attempted to relate their reactions when Harvey shifted his burden onto the janitor with instructions to dump it in the trash, and she deposited hers in the pastor's arms suggesting that it might be permanently placed on the chapel altar. They said they planned to share the expense of providing a new cross for the sanctuary. It was to be chosen by the Worship Taskforce and the Trustees.

Their chins really hit the floor, though, when Harvey held out his arm to Emma and asked her to join him for a cup of coffee, after which he would give her a ride home. No one was ever told just what had occurred in that elevator in those three and a half hours. But it had a lasting effect on Emma and Harvey, and on the church as well.

Who Is The Greatest?

*... he asked them, "What were you arguing about on the
way?" But they were silent, for on the way they had argued
with one another who was the greatest.*

— verses 33b-34

A holy woman from India was traveling through the United
States on a speaking tour to raise money for orphanages and
hospitals operated by her order. Two wealthy philanthropists
approached her with plans to donate very large sums of money.
One wanted to build a hospital for the poor. The other shared his
desire to open a chain of homeless shelters in several cities. When
the holy woman left the room, the two men got into a friendly
discussion about which of their donations would save the most lives.
A gentlemanly wager was discussed, with the loser agreeing to
donate a substantial sum to the winner's favorite charity. When the
holy woman returned, they asked if she would serve as a kind of
referee to determine which of them had won the wager.

The holy woman told them that she could not possibly make
that kind of determination, but she could show them a way to make
the determination themselves if they would follow her for one day.
The two philanthropists agreed. The holy woman took them to a
tiny apartment in one of the old neighborhoods of the city and
introduced them to a young man who was HIV-positive and living
with several AIDS-related illnesses. He had been hospitalized
several times and had escaped death twice. Now he was in remission
and able to go about his daily work. The holy woman and the two
philanthropists followed him as he shopped for groceries for an
elderly homebound couple. They watched as he took a turn playing
with children whose mother had to leave them home alone while
she worked because she was too poor to afford daycare. And they

looked on as he bathed and fed an AIDS patient who was too weak to care for himself.

At the end of the day, one of the men turned to the holy woman and said, "I wouldn't do what he does for a million dollars."

"Neither would he," the holy woman replied. "Neither would he."

Author's note:
This story was inspired by the ministry of Mother Teresa.

Proper 21
Mark 9:38-50

One Of These Little Ones

"If any of you put a stumbling block before one of these little ones who believe in me, it would be better for you if a great millstone were hung around your neck and you were thrown into the sea."

— verse 42

The patrolman heard three shots fired in rapid succession and started running toward the sound as fast as his middle-aged legs would carry him. He saw the gun first, laying on the ground next to a chain link fence, and then he saw the child lying in a pool of blood, face down on the sidewalk. He couldn't have been more than ten years old. The child had a faint pulse when the patrolman made the radio call for the ambulance, but he was dead within a few minutes.

The patrolman listened to the siren wail above the din of the traffic as he cradled the dead child's head in his lap. It was always the same. The investigation would reveal that the child got the gun from an older brother or a cousin who was a member of one of the neighborhood gangs. His parents would be shocked to hear that their baby had a gun, would deny that their good Christian son, who went to the corner church every Sunday and sang in the children's choir, could have pointed a loaded gun in anger at another boy. The patrolman had heard it all before. And that was why he would come back tonight — after he had weeded the flower garden in his backyard and wept for this child, and after he had tucked his own little children into their beds — to the basement of the church on the corner where community leaders met two nights a week, seeking ways to make the neighborhood safe for their children. Someday it would be different. Someday ....

Proper 22
Mark 10:2-16

What God Has Joined Together

" 'For this reason a man shall leave his father and mother
and be joined to his wife, and the two shall become one
flesh.' So they are no longer two, but one flesh. Therefore,
what God has joined together, let no one separate."

— verses 7-9

Laurie reached for the telephone for the third time in ten minutes, but, once again, her hand recoiled as soon as she touched it. She needed to talk to someone, but the very act of talking about what was eating away at her seemed wrong, as if voicing the problem would make it real. Then there could be no turning back. A part of her being screamed for that to happen, but another part resisted. Intellectually, Laurie knew that her life and her marriage were in crisis. Emotionally, she felt unable to deal with it.

Laurie tended to blame her ambivalence toward their marriage on Bob, but she couldn't pinpoint any particular incident or turning point. When she had married Bob, sixteen years earlier, they were in love and they shared goals which had been fulfilled, one at a time, more or less in order: getting their careers off the ground, buying the house, baby number one (a son named Jeremy), Bob's promotion, baby number two (a daughter named Betsy), Laurie's concentration on her freelance art work, as the children grew. House number one was traded for the custom-built dream house with a sunny studio for her painting. Then, somewhere between Jeremy's first day in kindergarten and Betsy's, life began to seem mundane.

Bob was very successful in his business career, but it took nearly all of his time and energy. Although he had always been a good father to their children — taking his turn with midnight feedings and floor walkings when they were tiny, making time for little league, dance recitals and school programs as they grew, sitting with them in church while she sang in the choir — he was sometimes

181

distant. When he wasn't shut up in his den evenings, working, he was often exercising to relieve stress. It wasn't that he cared less about Laurie and the children. It was more a matter of not having the energy and patience to expend on them. Laurie began to feel they had nothing left in common. She still loved him, but there was a widening gap in their relationship, and she grew tired of trying to find ways to bridge it. She missed the closeness — the romance of their courtship and early married years. They used to talk: to be in tune with one another. But years and careers and children seemed to dull the connection. Laurie longed for those old feelings, tried to bury her discontent in her artwork, spent more afternoons and evenings out with women friends, and spent days at a time feeling angry and frustrated. And then Jim moved in across the street.

She hadn't planned for it to happen. At first, she had only been curious about the new neighbor who had bought a four bedroom house just for himself and his dog. The first time Laurie met him, taking out the trash at the same time he was piling up packing cartons, she had thought him scruffy and more than a bit unclean. Then she found herself noticing the work he did on the house, the improvements he made in the yard, and the time he spent playing frisbee with his Black Lab. She began watching his comings and goings, "happened" to be outside when he mowed his lawn, and took him a glass of iced tea when he was painting the trim on his porch. They formed an easygoing, neighborly friendship, stopping their various chores to share coffee and conversation several times a week.

Jim was a freelance writer. He traveled periodically to cover boating events for a magazine on sailing. He owned a 25-foot cruising sailboat, on which he lived and often traveled to his assignments during the warm months. Jim was 47, had been divorced for seven years, and had two grown sons: one a musician and the other a law student at Yale. There were a number of young women who came and went from Jim's house at all hours of the day and night.

At first Laurie denied, even to herself, that she had anything but a friendly interest in Jim. He had fascinating stories to tell of ocean voyages and near disasters aboard his sailboat. He had traveled extensively, and his stories brought out a yearning Laurie had squelched years before. Tropical ports, sunny beaches, painting ocean sunsets, sailing under a full moon and diamond-studded sky: all of those things she had once considered romantic and desirable — before she was married — before she had children and responsibilities. It had been so long ago, before she knew that youth wouldn't last forever, that there were things that would never reach their "someday." She was 37 years old. That *wasn't* old. She didn't *feel* old — except when Bob closed himself up in his den at 7:00 and lilting female laughter and slamming car doors across the street reminded her that there were other possibilities in life. There was something more than washing someone else's favorite pair of jeans for school tomorrow and sitcoms on television to fill an evening.

Jim was not a flirtatious man. When their friendship had progressed beyond getting to know one another — when Laurie had dared to share some of her deepest wishes and desires for her life with him, and he had shared some of his with her — when her doubts about her life had surfaced and nearly overflowed onto him, although she had managed to hold them back, he had read them anyway. He understood. And he told her he would be there for her. He also let her know, in no uncertain terms, that he was determined never to marry again. His failed marriage and the break-up of his family had been one of the most devastating events in his life. He was positive that he would never put himself into that kind of position again. But if Laurie wanted to get away, all she had to do was say the word. He would gladly sail away to the tropics with her if she wanted to taste that life.

Laurie didn't know quite what to do. It became harder and harder to be with Bob, to sleep with him or have him touch her. They argued much more frequently, over very small things. She thought of Jim almost constantly. She dreamed about him. Although he had never made any physical advances toward her, she felt jealous of the women he dated. But, at the same time, Laurie knew there was nowhere to go. Jim would not marry her. He had no interest in her children. And Bob hadn't actually done anything wrong. They

183

had both just stopped doing things right. Perhaps when she distanced herself from him, he had taken it as permission to stop working on their relationship. Was he bored with her, too? And what about the children? At eight and ten, they were still very vulnerable. If she and Bob separated, if she went away, even for a short while, would the children be scarred for life? If they didn't separate, could she stand it? She was 37 years old, but she was still desirable to other men. She could tell that from Jim's attitude. He didn't need to say it in words. In another few years, would anyone care anymore? Would she lose all hope for real romance if she waited? But the words of her marriage vows echoed in her head: for better, for worse; for richer, for poorer; in sickness and in health … until death do us part.

Laurie reached for the phone. She had looked up the number so many times that she had it memorized. When it rang the first time she nearly hung up again, but the woman's voice that answered before a second ring stopped her. "Pastor Susan, this is Laurie Pope calling. Are you able to talk?"

"Yes, of course, Laurie. But you sound upset. Are you all right?"

"No. I really need to talk to someone."

"Would you like to come here, or would you like me to come there?" the pastor asked, and Laurie breathed a sigh of relief. "Please, come right over, Pastor Susan. Please, come as soon as you can. I need some advice right now."

She had done it; she had said it out loud. The problem was real. Now she — they — would have to deal with it.

Father Good

... a man ran up and knelt before him, and asked, "Good Teacher, what must I do to inherit eternal life?" Jesus said to him, "Why do you call me good? No one is good but God alone."

— verses 17-18

They called him Father Good, though he was not ordained and he had no natural children. His given name was Christopher Goodson. Everybody had called him Chris when he worked in the filling station uptown. But when he moved to the south side neighborhood, after Mildred died, the kids there started to call him Father Good. Chris said it was because he talked to them about spiritual things. But it was more than that. He was a father figure to a lot of kids who had had little attention from their own fathers, if they even knew who their fathers were.

Chris didn't much like the nickname. "I'm not so good," he used to tell the kids. "If Mildred was here she would set you straight. She knew what kind of guy I really am. And besides," he said, "the Bible says very clearly that only God is good. Jesus wouldn't even let them hang that one on him." But the nickname persisted despite, or perhaps because of, Chris' adamant protestations.

Chris loved two things in life after he lost Mildred: his flowers and all of those kids. He told me that it was on account of the kids that he moved to the south side. He said he was just driving around one day when he came upon this neighborhood with rundown houses and apartment buildings. He said there were broken bottles, pop cans, old tires, magazines and newspapers blowing in the alleys, hundreds of kids everywhere, and no sign of a tree or a flower within blocks. "That's no way for any child to grow up," Chris said. So he bought the first ramshackle house that came on the market and moved in.

185

The first thing Chris did was to clean up his own lawn. He hauled away all of the garbage, set out trees and put in several flower beds. He hired some of the kids to help him. When that was done they painted the house, and then he started on the rest of the block. Chris organized a neighborhood association. He got the alderman and the cops on the beat involved. Soon local business men and women were taking an interest. Storefronts were painted and parking lots resurfaced. Civic pride was catching. Suddenly there was money available from the city to fix streetlights and to repair curbs and gutters which had been crumbling for years.

The development of Reggie White Park, named after the NFL football hero who lent his support to the neighborhood association, was Chris' proudest achievement. It provided the kids with a safe place to play. Chris solicited funds throughout the city for playground equipment, basketball courts and a water fountain. He organized teams of kids to water the trees and flowers that he personally planted. It is a beautiful park, a source of pride for everyone on the south side. The last time I saw Chris, he was talking about raising money for scholarships so that some of the kids he loved would have a chance to go to college.

My job took me to another state after that. I lost track of Chris, except for an occasional Christmas card. He wasn't one to write much and neither am I. Still, I was shocked when a mutual friend called to tell me that Chris had died. I felt like I had lost one of my closest friends, even though we had not seen each other for fifteen years. It didn't seem possible that Chris was 93 years old. I learned that he had spent the last two years in a local nursing home.

I flew back for the funeral, wishing that I had had the good sense to visit while Chris was still alive. The funeral home was packed with Chris' neighbors and friends. I recognized many more people than I thought I would. But there were many well-dressed young men and women that I didn't remember, until they reminded me that we had met when I used to visit at Chris' house. They were all Chris' kids, come home to give thanks for the old man who had given them so much. They were teachers and lawyers and engineers and nurses and electricians and carpenters and independent business men and women. A few of them were raising their families in the old neighborhood and keeping it up as Chris had taught them. Many of them said they had been able to go on to school because Chris helped them to get scholarships.

When the preacher had finished with the sermon, he invited people to stand up and share their memories of Chris, and many did. One well-dressed young man, who was seated between his pretty young wife and his mother, stood up and, with tears in his eyes, said, "How I loved that old man, because he loved me and took care of me like no other man I ever knew. I don't know where I'd be today if it wasn't for Chris. God bless Father Good."

Frog Song

You who live in the shelter of the Most High, who abide in the shadow of the Almighty, will say to the Lord, "My refuge and my fortress; my God in whom I trust." For he will deliver you from the snare of the fowler and from the deadly pestilence; he will cover you with his pinions, and under his wings you will find refuge ...

Those who love me, I will deliver; I will protect those who know my name. When they call to me, I will answer them; I will be with them in trouble, I will rescue them and honor them. With long life I will satisfy them and show them my salvation.

— verses 1-4b, 14-16

"We will hear citizens' comments now," the Mayor announced. It was Monday night, and the weekly City Council meeting had just been called to order by his honor, Mayor Leland R. Steadman. The Council chambers became quiet as the aldermen and the one newly elected alderwoman settled into their high-backed, black leather swivel chairs for what most of them viewed as a wasted half-hour of citizen criticisms and complaints. It was always the same people with the same axes to grind, week after week. They had heard it all before ... or so they thought.

"Who's up first tonight?" the Mayor asked, looking at the secretary.

"Mrs. Gertrude Sommers of 1905 Marsh Lane," the secretary intoned.

A very old woman got up from a seat in the back of the chamber and hobbled toward the microphone. She was less than five feet tall; her back was bent and her shoulders rounded from osteoporosis. She was carrying a cane in one hand, which she wielded like a club, and she had a large shopping bag in the other. From the shopping bag she took a small, portable tape recorder, which she placed on the lectern under the microphone. Her large head, covered with curly, white hair and framed in pearl-rimmed glasses, was barely visible above the lectern. The cameraman had to raise his tripod and zoom down, so the citizens watching on the city cable channel at home could see all of her face. She reached up, pulled the microphone down to her level, and then boomed into it in a gruff voice that startled everyone in the Council chambers.

"Gentlemen ... and Lady," she began, nodding to the Council's only woman member, "I want you to hear something." She switched on the tape recorder and the Council chamber was filled with the sounds of hundreds of frogs, singing at the tops of their voices. Mrs. Sommers let the tape go on for a couple of minutes. The Council members exchanged amused glances. This was something new! "That was five years ago," Mrs. Sommers said as she stopped the tape. "It was recorded in the marshland, along the lake, across the road from my house. This is what it sounds like today." She switched the tape recorder on again. This time there was a long silence, interrupted occasionally by the call of a whipporwill and the faint sound of a dog barking in the distance — but there were no frog sounds. Mrs. Sommers let the tape play on and on until she could see that the Council members were becoming annoyed. Then she turned it off, pulled herself up to her full height, and speaking in a measured tone, as she moved her eyes slowly from one Council member to another, she said, "Gentlemen ... and Lady, what has happened to the frogs? Where have they gone? That's all I want to know. What has happened to our frogs?" The Council members' amused glances became surprised and confused as the old woman turned abruptly and hobbled back to her seat without another word.

The next citizen up that night was Carson Peters. He was a tall, stringy man about the same age as Mrs. Sommers. He had to bend over to speak into the microphone. "I'm a neighbor of Mrs. Sommers," he announced, and the Council quickly understood that this was the second wave of the frog assault. "I've been living near the marsh on the lake for over seventy years. I grew up there, and me and the wife, we raised our kids there. The frogs have always been a part of our lives. We watched for the tadpoles first thing in the spring, and we went to sleep listening to the frogs sing every summer night. A few years ago, we noticed that there weren't as many frogs singing as there used to be. Gradually, they have disappeared altogether. We haven't heard any frogs singing for over a year. I miss the frogs. I don't sleep well anymore." He sat down, and the Council members were relieved when the rest of the comments continued in the normal vein.

But the next week they were back again, Mrs. Sommers and Mr. Peters. This time they had photographs of frogs in the marshland along the lake as they appeared five years ago — eight by ten blow-ups of big frogs, little frogs, tadpoles, pollywogs, and frog spawn. Mr. Peters passed the pictures around for the Council members to examine while Mrs. Sommers narrated. Then, taking out another set of photographs, she said, "This is what the marshland looks like today." The Council members could see that the photographs showed the same landmarks, the same languid pools of water, accented here and there by cattails and swamp grasses, but no frogs. "I challenge you," said Mrs. Sommers, "to find one frog anywhere in that marsh. Gentlemen, and Lady, what has happened to the frogs?"

Mr. Peters collected the photographs and the two were about to return to their seats when Councilwoman Mary Ellen Perry said, "Mrs. Sommers, Mr. Peters, we all share your concern about the frogs. Their disappearance from our marshlands is, indeed, very disturbing. But, honestly, what do you want us to do?"

"We want to know what has happened to the frogs," Mrs. Sommers said. "What has caused them to disappear? It's not just that we love the frogs and miss their songs; we want to know what has happened to the frogs, lest what happened to them should also happen to us."

Two weeks passed, and neither Mrs. Sommers nor Mr. Peters appeared during citizens' comments time to ask about the frogs. The Council members thought they had seen the last of them, but on the third week they were back again, and with them was a youngish-looking fellow wearing a navy blue blazer and a red silk tie. Several sarcastic comments could be heard as the Council members watched them come in and take their seats.

"Here come the frog people again!"

"Oh, no! What are they going to do this time?"

"Wonder who the new guy is? Looks like he dressed for the camera."

When their turn came, Mrs. Sommers wasted no time in introducing their guest. "This is Dr. David Bradfort," she said, addressing the Council members. "He is Professor of Environmental Studies at the University. He is going to tell you what has happened to the frogs, and what you ought to be doing about it."

Professor Bradfort stepped up to the microphone, opened a black folder, glanced down at his notes, then gazed resolutely at the Council members as he spoke. "What Mrs. Sommers and Mr. Peters have been telling you about the disappearance of the frogs is true, and it's not just happening here in our community; it is happening all around the world. I attended a workshop in Irvine, California, in February of 1990, in which the decline of amphibians was discussed by forty different scientists from all over the world. They all agreed that amphibian species are declining at an alarming rate, some, apparently, to the point of extinction.

"Although scientists usually prefer to wait until all of the data is in before reaching any conclusions, there has been a sense of urgency in scientific journals during the past several months. One quoted Dr. David Wake, the organizer of the conference, as saying:

Amphibians were here when the dinosaurs were here, and they survived the age of the mammals. They are tough survivors. If they are checking out now I think it is significant.

Dr. Bradfort looked up from his notes and said, "It gets worse. Other articles suggest that this trend may point to greater environmental problems. Amphibians could be an early warning system, signalling imbalances or advanced breakdowns in the environment. There isn't much evidence that there is a single, global cause for the decline, but the conference panelists suggested potential localized causes may include destruction of the natural habitat, pesticide pollution, and acid rain. Increases in ultraviolet rays and higher temperatures due to global warming through holes in the ozone layer might also explain the global effect. Both believers and skeptics agreed that immediate, long-term studies are needed, but they might be a luxury we can't afford. The results may come too late. One scientist has suggested short-term experiments, like reintroducing the species and conducting intensive studies of its fate.

"That's what I think we should do here in our community: introduce some frogs of the same species as those that used to live in the marsh, then observe them closely to determine what it is that now prevents frogs from surviving in that environment. I warn you, though, that if we undertake such a study, you may find the results disturbing."

With that Dr. Bradfort closed his black book and sat down. No one said anything for several moments. The Mayor, the Council members, and everyone else in the Council chambers looked stunned. Finally, Alderwoman Mary Ellen Perry broke the silence. "Your honor, I move that we authorize Professor Bradfort to begin an immediate study of environmental conditions in the marshland near the lake, and that we allocate $10,000.00 to pay for it." The resolution passed without debate.

The following morning, Professor David Bradfort appeared at the marsh with a University van loaded with frogs, cameras, microscopes, a variety of scientific measuring equipment, and a tent in which he intended to live until the study was complete. He let the frogs loose and settled in for a long stay. Night and day he observed the frogs, often forgetting to eat and sleep. His dissecting, testing, measuring, and the recording of his findings in his journal became an obsession. He would not let up until he knew what was killing the frogs and what might be done to save them from extinction.

Just after dusk on the fortieth day, he was lying on a sleeping bag by the fire in front of his tent, exhausted from the long hours of work and lack of proper nourishment. Some of his scientist friends would say later that what happened next was an hallucination: the result of an hypoglycemic episode brought on by his hunger. But David insists to this day that what he experienced was a true vision.

He says that she appeared to him rising on the mist that filled the night air: a Great Mother frog, her spotted green coat glistening in the moonlight. Her large, unblinking amphibian eyes seemed to be filled with fire and light. He felt as if she were looking straight through him, deep into his soul. And then she addressed him in his own language.

"O Human One," she croaked in her deep, frog voice, "you are hungry. My legs are tender and sweet. Take and eat. I give them to you."

"Oh, no," he said, "I couldn't hurt you. And besides, how would you live without your legs?"

"The Most High will take care of me. We have an understanding. Take and eat. You must eat or you will die."

So David took the legs of the Great Mother frog. He roasted them over the fire and ate of the tender, sweet meat until he was full and his strength had returned. Then he cut strips of cloth from his shirt and bound up the Great Mother's wounds. "Now," he said, "you must allow me to give something of myself to you. O Great Mother frog, what do you need that I can give?"

The Great Mother thought for a moment, and then she said, "If you will listen to my song and promise to sing it wherever you go, I will count it as a blessing and call you friend for as long as I live."

"I will listen," David said, "and I promise to sing your song wherever I go."

Then the Great Mother frog opened her mouth and began to sing:

> We who live in the shelter of the Most High,
> creatures of both land and sea,
> we do not fear the poison falling in the rain,
> or the two-legged ones who drain our marshes and ponds,
> we sing for the Great One, our refuge and our strength,
> we remember the promise and we sing.

> Chorus: You who love me, I will deliver,
> I will save all those who know my name,
> when you call to me I will answer,
> sing your songs, sing your songs,
> live long and free.

When she had finished her song the Great Mother looked up toward the sky and croaked loud and deep, "Come for me." In the blink of an eye a golden eagle swooped down from the sky, grasped the Great Mother frog in his talons, and winged off with her held gently, but firmly, in his grasp. As they flew off together through the night, the Great Mother called out, "Human One, remember my song."

The following Monday night, Professor David Bradfort was back in the City Council chambers to give a preliminary report on his study of environmental conditions in the marshland along the lake. The Mayor and the Council members greeted him warmly and waited eagerly to hear what he had to say. He told them in precise scientific terms the nature of the poisons that had killed the frogs. He named the factories in the community that were dumping pollutants into the lake and emitting toxins. He reminded them of the number of automobiles and trucks that were spewing exhaust fumes into the air and the enormous amounts of toxic chemicals being sprayed on fields and lawns to kill weeds and insects.

"It's not surprising," he told them, "that the frogs have all died. It is amazing that they survived as long as they did. What is surprising is that it has taken us so long to notice, because the same poisons that killed the frogs are killing us, too. The passing of the frogs is a sign for us — a warning before it is too late."

And then, right there in front of the Mayor and the City Council members, and live and in color for the citizens watching the city cable channel at home, Professor Bradfort told about his vision. And he opened his mouth wide — as wide as the big-mouthed Great Mother frog — and began to sing her song.

Author's note:

"Frog Song" was inspired by an article which appeared in *The New York Times*, February 20, 1990. "Scientists Confront An Alarming Mystery: The Vanishing Frog" by Sandra Blakeslee tells of a panel of 22 experts convened by the National Research Council, a non-profit organization that advises the government on scientific matters. Dr. David Bradford, Professor of Environmental Studies at the University of California at Los Angeles, said the group drafted an emergency letter to the world's scientists calling their attention to the immediacy of the problem. Dr. Bradford referred us to several articles which were a further basis for the story. These included, "Where Have All The Froggies Gone," from the March 2, 1990, edition of *Science*; the *Bulletin of the Ecological Society of America*, June, 1990, Volume 71, No. 2; "Where Have All the Frogs and Toads Gone?" by Kathryn Phillips in *BioScience*, Volume 40 No. 6, June, 1990. An editorial in the same volume recommended "... the immediate marshalling of a major biodiversity project, on the scale of the Human Genome Project or even larger. The survival of our planet as we know it may be in the balance." For more information write to the Environmental Science and Emergency Program, School of Public Health, 10833 Le Conte Avenue, UCLA, Los Angeles, CA 90024-1772. Phone 213-825-0998.

John told this story in the closing worship of The Fellowship of United Methodists in Worship, Music and Other Arts Convocation at Lake Junaluska, NC, July 19, 1991.

The music for "Frog Song" was composed by Kerri Sherwood, Director of Music at First United Methodist Church in Kenosha, WI. Ms. Sherwood's new CD of original solo piano music, *Released From The Heart*, is available from Sisu music, PO Box 1945, Kenosha, WI 53141.

Proper 25
Mark 10:46-52

Will Work For Food

Immediately he gained his sight and followed him on the way.

— verse 52b

A well-known politician came into a large American city one day to speak at a political rally. He was running for President and his campaign was gaining more and more momentum each day.

As the politician made his way along the edge of the crowd, on the way to the speaker's platform, he came upon a man carrying a sign with large, red letters which read, "WILL WORK FOR FOOD." The man called out to the politician in a loud voice, "Mr. President, help me, I need a job!" The politician's aides and others sternly ordered the man to be quiet, but he hollered out even more loudly, "Mr. President, help me. I need a job!"

The politician stopped and said, "Tell him to come over here." His aides went to the man and said, "This is your lucky day. The candidate will speak to you. Be careful what you say."

The unemployed man dropped his sign and came immediately to talk to the politician. The politician asked, "What can I do for you, sir?"

The unemployed man replied, "Mr. President, I need a job. I am willing to do anything to feed my family."

The politician said to him, "Your persistence and your willingness to do anything to feed your family are an inspiration. You shall have a job!"

The unemployed man smiled, reached out and shook the politician's hand and said, "I accept. When do I go to work?"

A film of this strange exchange with the unemployed man was made into a campaign commercial for the politician, which was credited with launching him to the Presidency. After his inauguration, he gave the formerly unemployed man a job as a lobbyist for the Labor Department.

Deuteronomy 6:1-9; Hebrews 9:11-14

Laying Down The Law

Now this is the commandment — the statutes and the ordinances— that the Lord your God charged me to teach you to observe in the land you are about to cross into and occupy, so that you and your children and your children's children, may fear the Lord your God all the days of your life, and keep all his decrees and his commandments that I am commanding you, so that your days may be long.
— Deuteronomy 6:1-2

But when Christ came as a high priest of the good things that have come ... he entered once for all into the Holy Place, not with the blood of goats and calves, but with his own blood, thus obtaining eternal redemption.
— Hebrews 9:11-12

Awards Sunday was the biggest annual event at Calvary Church. Every year the best and the brightest and the most persistent of the Sunday School children lined up in the front of the sanctuary to receive their pins for memorizing Bible verses and books of the Bible, writing essays on selected scriptural passages, perfect attendance and community service. The community service award was given to the student who was most Christ-like in his or her service to the community. It was usually given to one of the high school kids and was the most coveted award.

There were 11 recipients of perfect attendance awards this year, and Tammy Lee Hartley, the superintendent's daughter, was to receive her six-year pin. Tammy had been asked to give a brief speech in hopes that she might inspire some of the other children to increase their efforts. The speech went well enough, though a bit too long. Tammy's parents and grandparents beamed with pride and the church elders looked on approvingly. The first graders had lined up in front and were midway through the first verse of "Jesus Loves Me" when suddenly there was a big boom that echoed throughout the sanctuary. The base of one of the candles on the altar had exploded and the candle had taken off toward the ceiling like a rocket. It bounced off a beam and then, as it fell back toward the floor, came to rest on one of the crossbars of the cross which hung directly over the altar. Three seventh grade boys in the fourth row burst out laughing. Everyone else sat in stunned silence.

The superintendent and the pastor made a beeline for the seventh grade boys, who had been troublemakers all year long. Billy Packer was the ringleader. He was continually pulling pranks on his teachers and classmates. The superintendent and the pastor herded Billy into the Sunday School office and prepared to give him the third degree. Billy readily admitted that he was responsible for the candle explosion, but he was clearly unrepentant. The pastor and the superintendent were about to lay down the law when they were interrupted by a firm knock on the door. It was the seventh grade Sunday School teacher, Steve Dexter. Steve asked if they would be willing to turn the job of disciplining Billy over to him. He said, "I think I know just what is needed." The pastor and the superintendent were a little reluctant because they both believed that Steve was too lenient with his class. But they agreed to give him a chance since he was Billy's teacher. Steve said he would meet with Billy and his parents after the awards ceremony. He whispered something in Billy's ear as they walked back toward the sanctuary. Billy's face turned pale. He looked like he might run away any minute. Steve draped his arm around Billy's shoulder and kept him going in the right direction.

As they entered the sanctuary, the fifth graders were just finishing a new rap version of the the Twenty-third Psalm. Then came the highlight of the awards ceremony, the presentation of the community service award. The superintendent announced that the presentation would be made by the teacher of the student who was to receive the award. Steve Dexter got up and walked up to the front. Before he spoke he motioned to someone in the back to come forward and join him at the microphone. A tired-looking, middle-aged man in a wheelchair began to make his way slowly up the aisle. Billy Packer slid down as low as he could get in the pew and covered his face with his hands. Then came the announcement everyone was waiting for. "This year's winner of the community service award," Steve said, "is Billy Packer." There was a communal gasp of surprise from the congregation, and then a spattering of polite applause. Everyone was stunned, almost as much as they had been when the candle exploded. They began to murmur among themselves. How could a troublemaker like Billy Packer win the community service award?

Steve Dexter leaned over toward the man in the wheelchair and handed him the microphone. Everyone became very quiet as the man began to speak. "Most of you don't know me," he intoned in a a raspy voice. "I haven't been able to come to church for a long, long time. But a few of you might recall that I won the community service award in 1969 when I was a senior." There were a few slow nods of recognition. "I am very proud," the man went on, "to be given the honor of presenting this year's award to my nephew, Billy Packer. Billy gave me one of his kidneys. He was the only person in our family whose DNA was the right match for mine. It is because of Billy's gift that I am still alive today. I want to thank him for saving my life, and thank all of you in this church for helping Billy learn to give of himself like Christ did." Then Billy's uncle handed the microphone back to Steve. This time the applause was loud and sustained.

Steve said, "Now, I would like to ask Billy to come up and say a few words." Billy, with his head still hanging low, made his way slowly to the microphone. In a weak, halting voice he began, "I don't think I deserve to get any award, especially after what I did with the candle. I just want to say that I'm sorry and I will never do anything like that again." Then he looked at his uncle and said, "I don't think what I did was such a big deal. I just love Uncle Jim and I want him to be well."

Steve hugged Billy and pushed him toward his Uncle Jim for another embarrassing hug. The pianist launched into "Amazing Grace" and the awards ceremony was over for another year. Several months passed before anyone bothered to remove the candle which had landed on the crossbar of the cross.

Giving All

"Truly I tell you, this poor widow has put in more than all
of those who are contributing to the treasury. For all of
them have contributed out of their abundance; but she
out of her poverty has put in everything she had, all she
had to live on."

— verses 43b-44

Gerald Fitzgerald was the biggest giver at First Redeemer
Church. Fitz, as he was called, was the owner of his own business
and well-known for his generosity. Because of this, he had often
been called on by the leaders in the congregation to head up the
annual pledge drive. One year, while going over the pledges from
the previous year, Fitz was surprized to discover that the second
biggest pledge in the church was almost as much as his pledge.
Fitz didn't recognize the name of the pledger, so when it was time
to assign the callers for visitation Sunday, he added Midge
Griswold's name to the list of persons that he would personally
call on.

Fitz was curious about who Midge was. No one on his committee
had recognized her name. The pastor said she was a new member
who had joined the congregation the year before. Fitz looked
forward to meeting Midge. He thought she must be quite a wealthy
woman if she was able to give almost as much he did. Perhaps she
was an older woman who had inherited money from her husband
or her family. She must live in a grand house in a nice neighborhood.
Maybe he and his wife could invite her over for dinner sometime.
If she was new in the church, she might welcome an opportunity to
meet some of the congregation's leaders.

When Fitz pulled up in front of a small apartment building,
which, according to his directions, was where Midge lived, he
checked the address twice to make sure he was at the right place.

She must own the building, Fitz thought to himself. He told the young woman who answered the door of the very modest apartment that he was looking for Mrs. Griswold. "I'm Midge Griswold," the young woman replied. "What can I do for you?" Fitz was so taken aback that he almost forgot why he had come. But finally he managed to tell her that he was from the church and he had come to pick up her pledge for the next year. "Oh, of course," Midge said, "I've been expecting you. Come and sit down while I fill it out."

Fitz noticed a picture of an older couple on the end table and he asked Midge who they were. "They are my grandparents," Midge said. "They are missionaries in Haiti. That's where I grew up. Grandpa and Grandma raised me after my folks died." Midge handed Fitz her pledge card. She hadn't bothered to put it in an envelope, so Fitz couldn't help but see that Midge's pledge for the next year was substantial. Indeed, it was considerably more than his own. Fitz couldn't help himself. He was startled. How could such a young woman with apparently modest means afford to give so much? Fitz wasn't ordinarily a nosy person, but in this instance he couldn't help himself; he had to know.

"Miss Griswold," Fitz began in a more formal voice than he intended, "I am curious about your pledge." Immediately a look of great concern came over Midge's face and before Fitz could go on to explain himself, she interrupted him and said, "I hope it's enough. I know I'm not giving as much as I should. Nurses make good money here, but the cost of living is so much higher than it is in Haiti. I can't seem to give any more than a tithe. I'm hoping to do better next year. The need in the world is so great, and our church does so much good. I want to help all I can."

"Oh, don't worry," Fitz said. "You're doing just fine. We are very fortunate to have you as a part of our congregation."

With that, Fitz bid Midge a hasty good-bye and left as quickly as he could. He was deeply troubled by Midge's generosity. How can she live like that, Fitz wondered? Giving so much — it's not practical. But what troubled him most was how much he was going to have to raise his own pledge.

The Lord Always Before Me:
Lavinda's Christmas Letter

*I keep the Lord always before me; because he is at my
right hand, I shall not be moved. Therefore my heart is
glad, and my soul rejoices; my body also rests secure.
For you do not give me up to Sheol, or let your faithful
one see the Pit. You show me the path of life. In your
presence there is fullness of joy; in your right hand are
pleasures forevermore.*

— verses 8-11

Christmas, 1979

Dear Ones:

From May 7 until June 11, 1979, it was my pleasure to spend
35 days travelling and visiting in the northwest United States, using
a Greyhound Ameripass. So many events with inspirational
implications happened that the desire to share some of them with
you results in this letter.

The bus moved effortlessly across the rolling hills of Minnesota,
onto the seemingly neverending plains of South Dakota, until we
reached the southwest corner of the Black Hills. Leaving Rapid
City at twilight, we rode for miles through an unroofed tunnel
flanked on each side with rows of the dark pines pointing toward
the sky with their tops like church spires. I couldn't help but sing
the words of Henry Van Dyke's beautiful hymn in my head:

*All thy works with joy surround thee,
Earth and heaven reflect Thy rays;
Stars and angels sing around Thee,
Center of unbroken praise.*

Field and forest, vale and mountain
Flowery meadows, flashing sea;
Chanting birds and flowing fountain,
Call us to rejoice in Thee.

As the darkness deepened, snatches of a sky sprinkled with stars, as mentioned in the song, could be caught by looking through the upper part of the bus window.

Two days later, we travelled over a highway arched over by the branches of trees with a ceiling of leaves. These were Van Dyke's forest. As the bus followed the highway skirting the Idaho Rocky Mountains, we glimpsed, between the mountain peaks, the valleys below, with small fields of hay and grain — land which has been reclaimed through irrigation, and which also fit the hymn.

The flowery meadows we found in British Columbia, where the apple orchards were in full bloom. One could picture these same branches laden with ripened fruit in the fall. A visit to Kootenay Park gave us an imaginary "flashing sea." A river flowing swiftly down a low gorge was tunneled through a large tile. The water pulsed and protested as it plunged through the tile to tumble out the other side and fall with a noisy splash into the deeper gorge, which had been worn away by the force of the constantly flowing water.

Van Dyke's flowing fountains came to us in the form of the large, circular watering devices which shot high spouts of irrigation water into the air to water the farm lands. The water had come from the cooled and condensed steam from the hot springs which lie in the area near Twin Falls, Idaho.

Everywhere I went I encountered God's helpers who went beyond the call of duty to help me, proving that "Father love is reigning o'er us, Brother love binds man to man." There was the bus driver who directed me to a hotel in Mankato, Minnesota. And when I had registered at the Downtown Inn, another resident volunteered to take my suitcase and show me to my room. There was the ticket agent in Spokane, Washington, who, after he had asked if I was interested in luxury, or comfort and cleanliness, directed me to a hotel a block from the bus station. Here I had the least expensive night's lodging of the entire trip when using commercial accommodations. In Cheyenne, Wyoming, the ticket agent had not been of the same helpful disposition, so I went hunting alone. However, I met a young man who was from New York City and, when I asked him to help me, he walked with me to a nearby hotel. The next day this kind stranger treated me to a Mother's Day lunch in the hotel dining room. He told me I reminded him of his mother. I didn't have the heart to tell him I wasn't a mother.

But the "second miler" who surpassed them all was in Kansas City, Missouri. It was about ten o'clock at night of the day that my Ameripass ticket was due to run out. I had to change bus stations from Trailways to Greyhound. I stood at the curb to hail a cab when a man came rushing out of the station, looked at me and asked if I wanted a cab. When one came, he told the cab driver that he wanted to go to a beer parlor on the west side, but that he was to take me to the Greyhound bus station first. He put me in the back seat and then sat with the driver in the front. At the Greyhound station he told the driver to wait and, not giving me time to do anything about paying for my fare, he took my suitcase and headed into the station. I followed all the way to the ticket counter, where he put my suitcase down. I said, "God bless you for your kindness." He put an arm around my shoulder, kissed me on the cheek and whispered, "Take good care of yourself," and was gone.

I hope something in my account of this trip has brought you joy. May this joy, combined with the joys which this season represents, be a time of special blessings which will continue and carry through the year of 1980.

Laurinda

Author's note:

Laurinda Hampton was a retired United Methodist missionary. She was a teacher, and then an administrator, at The Harwood School for Girls in Albuquerque, New Mexico, until her retirement in 1969. Prior to her missionary work, she taught history and served as a librarian in Wauwatosa and Lancaster, Wisconsin, high schools. Miss Hampton was a member of Cargill United Methodist Church and a resident of Cedar Crest Retirement Community in Janesville, Wisconsin, at the time of her death on Memorial Day, 1989, at the age of 86. For many of her friends and students Laurinda Hampton embodied the love of Christ. Her gentle and powerful life-changing witness touched the hearts of many and will long be remembered in all of the communities where she lived and served.

Our thanks to her niece, Virginia McCartney, of Mount Hope, Wisconsin, for permission to share her story.

Christ the King
John 18:33-38

The Trial Of Gilbert Gunderson

*Then Pilate entered the headquarters again, summoned
Jesus, and asked him, "Are you the King of the Jews?" ....*

*Jesus answered, "You say that I am a King. For this I was
born, and for this I came into the world, to testify to the
truth. Everyone who belongs to the truth listens to my
voice."*

— verses 33, 37b

Gilbert Gunderson has been the editor of the Willow Bluff
weekly newspaper for as long as I, and everybody I know, can
remember. Gilbert inherited *The Free Press* from his father, old
Jack Gunderson, who, according to local lore, was reputed to have
won it in a card game sometime around the turn of the century. To
hear Gilbert tell it, the old man was never sure that he had gotten
such a good deal in the long run. *The Free Press*, in both old Jack's
and Gilbert's time, was never very profitable, but it had always
been known as an honest, no-nonsense newspaper. "We print the
truth, the whole truth and nothing but the truth," old Jack used to
say, and Gilbert had carried on the tradition, though sometimes it
had cost him readers and advertising revenue.

One community leader, in the midst of an enthusiastic
introduction at the annual Lincoln Day Dinner, had referred to
Gilbert as "the conscience of Willow Bluff." Gilbert had quickly
demurred, saying, "I'm not anybody's conscience. I just try to
provide accurate information so that everyone can decide what is
right." The truth was probably somewhere in between these two
extremes. Gilbert's blistering editorials were certainly more than
"accurate information." He used every bit of his considerable
persuasive power to convince his readers of the truth of certain
ideas that were contrary to their prejudices.

I was surprised, then, that day not long after Gilbert became ill, when he declared that he had been a failure as a father and a newspaperman. He said, "When it counted the most for my family and this community, I was silent." I knew he was depressed about his lung cancer, and so I didn't ask him to elaborate. At that point, we were optimistic that the cancer could be contained by the radiation and chemotherapy treatments.

There was a smell of cleaning chemicals in the air as I walked down the long hospital corridor toward Gilbert's room. He had sounded urgent on the phone. "Get over here right now!" That was the way he always talked to us when he passed out assignments at the paper. But this was different; it was personal and I feared the worst.

Gilbert was propped up on a pillow with IVs in each arm and tubes trailing off to monitors on both sides of the bed. He looked pale and painfully thin, but the smile and the hearty hello were vintage Gilbert. All that was missing was the trademark cigarette dangling from his lip. It was the three packs a day of these "detestable cancer sticks," as Gilbert called them, that had brought him to this "deep, dark abyss into which every mortal is fated to plunge." That was another "Gilbertism" that all of us had heard him spout often down at the office.

"Get out your pad and pencil," Gilbert commanded, "I've got a story for you to print before I die. When I'm dead, the paper will be yours and you can print anything you please."

This was Gilbert's way of telling me he was leaving me the paper. It was all I could do to hold back my tears and keep myself from hugging him. Gilbert knew how much *The Free Press* meant to me. It was his way of telling me he loved me. He had treated me like a son ever since the death of his own son after the war. But Gilbert was not one for hugs, even in these dire circumstances, so I dutifully took out my pad and pencil.

"I dreamed that I died last night," Gilbert began, "and I found myself in a great judgment hall, standing before Christ himself. He was seated on an alabaster throne and dressed in a translucent white robe that was trimmed in a shimmering substance that sparkled like diamonds. There was a gold crown on his head and he held a

209

silver scepter in his right hand. The Book of Life was spread out before him on a low table carved from the wood of a melaleuca alternifolia tree. The sweet fragrance of the melaleuca tree's healing oils filled the hall."

Gilbert loved to use obscure words and phrases that sent the rest of us scrambling for our dictionaries and encyclopedias. And he was a stickler for detail, so I struggled to get down every word.

Gilbert took a slow, painful breath and went on, "Christ pointed to the book of life and said, 'I see here that you are a newspaper editor and your name is Gilbert Gunderson. Is that true?'

" 'Yes, my Lord, I am Gilbert Gunderson.'

" 'Yes, yes, a very good record, indeed,' Christ said as he glanced down the page. 'But there is this one matter of the chemical company.'

"Christ looked up from the book and looked me square in the eye.

" 'It seems you knew about the danger of the chemicals produced there, but you wrote nothing to warn the public in your newspaper. It says here that you had seen a State Department report showing that these chemicals caused cancer in adults and birth defects in children.'

" 'Yes, I knew the chemicals were dangerous. But, the town needed the jobs. That chemical company paid the first decent wages that the people of Willow Bluff had seen since World War II, and they provided health and pension benefits. It brought economic stability to Willow Bluff, probably saved the town. I doubt if there would be anything left of Willow Bluff today if it hadn't been for that chemical company, and the Vietnam War. I figured that since the chemicals were being used to defoliate the jungles in the war effort, maybe it wouldn't hurt if no one knew what they were making. I would have been crucified if I had published one bad word about that chemical company. No one would have advertised in my paper and everyone else would have canceled their subscriptions. It would have been the end of *The Free Press*.'

" 'I see,' Christ said. 'And I see here that thousands of American veterans who fought in that war, and thousands of Vietnamese soldiers and civilians, have died as a result of cancers caused by exposure to these chemicals. It says that your own son, Jack, was one of those who died. Is that true?'

"It was at that point I woke up in a cold sweat with my body trembling from head to foot. I didn't get a wink of sleep the rest of the night."

Gilbert looked at me with tears in his eyes and said, "I cannot carry this burden of guilt to my grave. I must tell the community of my sin. It was wrong of me to keep silent. Write it all down: the dream, Jack's death, the huge profits the chemical company earned from selling their death potions to the Defense Department, the pressures from the leaders of this community to ignore what the chemical company was doing, my complicity in keeping the secret; write it all and print it on the front page in this week's edition. Go to the library; look up Agent Orange. It's all there."

Gilbert dismissed me with a wave of his hand and I knew there was no more to be said. I headed to the library and set to work. One of the best resources I found was a book called *My Father, My Son* by Admiral Elmo Zumwalt, Jr., and his son, Lieutenant Elmo Zumwalt III. The blurb on the dustcover said:

> ... *Elmo volunteered for one of the most dangerous Vietnam missions, commanding swift boats that patrolled rivers and canals. It was along these very rivers that Agent Orange, approved by his father in an effort to save Navy lives, was sprayed. Elmo miraculously survived to marry his college sweetheart, begin a successful law practice in North Carolina, and father two children. Then in 1983, he found he had cancer. He, and his father, believe it was Agent Orange that caused his cancer as well as severe learning disabilities in his son. Elmo tried to beat the odds with painful chemotherapy and bone-marrow transplants ....*

Elmo succumbed to the cancer not long after the book was published. The Zumwalts discovered in their research, during their vain attempts to save his life, that Agent Orange is a potent herbicide ..."as devastating to foilage as DDT is to insects."

The chemical itself is a fifty-fifty mixture of two herbicides,
2,4-D and 2,4,5-T. A third element, dioxin, which is an
extremely toxic chemical, was found as a contaminate in
Agent Orange, apparently as a product of the production
process itself ... Eleven chemical companies were involved
in defoliant production, including some major ones such
as Monsanto, Dow, Diamond, Shamrock, Hercules, and
North American Philips. (p. 235) ... investigations have
revealed that some of the chemical companies knew at the
time of the State Department's report that evidence existed
indicating 2,4,5-T caused birth defects in animals. And when
evidence was later published suggesting there were
potentially serious health hazards with this chemical, the
companies denied it ... As one Food and Drug
Administration researcher reported, dioxin would be as
potent a cause of birth defects as thalidomide. (p.236)

It was all starting to fit together. I knew now why Gilbert felt so guilty. I read on ...

As reports about Agent Orange's potential hazards
mounted, and congressional hearings brought additional
pressure to bear, this country discontinued spraying Agent
Orange in Vietnam in April 1970. (p. 237)

The Zumwalts quoted a Swedish study by Dr. Lennart Hardell which was published in *The British Journal of Cancer*:

... it suggests in summary, that exposure to organic
solvents, chlorophenols and/or phenoxy acids (2,4,5-T)
constituted a risk factor for the incidence of malignant
lymphoma ... (p. 237)

This was the final piece in the puzzle. I knew what had caused the untimely death of Gilbert's son and my best friend, Jack Gunderson. Jack had served in the same area in Vietnam as Lieutenant Zumwalt. He had been discharged in January of 1970 and had died of lymphoma cancer in 1987, the same year the Zumwalts book was published.

I wrote it all up, and then I paid a visit to our local chemical company. They admitted manufacturing Agent Orange in the late 1960s, but they refused to comment on what they called "any alleged toxic effects."

There was enough for a story without their cooperation. I set it up for the front page, and then I took it over to the hospital to show Gilbert. I was surprised to find that his condition was much worse than when I had seen him earlier in the day. He was flat on his back, his eyes were closed, and there was an oxygen mask over his nose. Gilbert opened his eyes when I took his hand. He motioned for me to remove his mask. The attending nurse, who had been adjusting his IVs, nodded her approval. Gilbert thanked me for coming. I started to tell him what I had discovered at the library, but he put his fingers to his lips and said, "Get out your pad and pencil." I quickly complied.

"I had another dream while you were gone," Gilbert said, "although this time I think it was more like the real thing."

I realized Gilbert was trying to tell me that he had had a near death experience.

"I felt myself slipping away," he said, "floating upwards out of my body and through a long tunnel toward a bright light. My son, Jack, and my father came to meet me. They embraced me and told me how glad they were to see me. I hugged them and heard myself laughing out loud in utter and complete joy. Then Jesus came and took my hand. I have never felt such peace in my whole life. He said, "We've been waiting for you, Gilbert. It is time for you to rest. But first you must go back and say good-bye to your friend. That's when you came in," Gilbert said, smiling up at me.

Then, with uncharacteristic tenderness, Gilbert said, "Now, give us a kiss and let this old man die in peace."

I kissed him and hugged him for a long time. The next day, my story about Gilbert's dreams, his silence about Agent Orange, and the cause of Jack's death appeared on the front page of *The Free Press* in the column next to his obituary. I printed every word, just as he told me, except the part about the kiss. That would always be mine to keep.

Admiral Elmo Zumwalt, Jr., and Lieutenant Elmo Zumwalt III, *My Father, My Son* (Boston: G.K. Hall & Co., 1987).

Appendix

The following pages contain five additional stories based on
lectionary texts in Cycle B. These stories are particularly appropriate for dealing with certain sensitive situations which a pastor
and congregation might encounter in today's society.

Luke 1:26-38, 47-55

Favor With God

In the sixth month the angel Gabriel was sent by God to a town in Galilee called Nazareth, to a virgin engaged to a man whose name was Joseph, of the house of David. The virgin's name was Mary. And he came to her and said, "Greetings favored one! The Lord is with you." But she was much perplexed by his words and pondered what sort of greeting this might be. The angel said to her, "Do not be afraid, Mary, for you have found favor with God. And now, you will conceive in your womb and bear a son ...."

— verses 26-31a

... you shall say to my servant David: Thus says the Lord of hosts: I took you from the pasture, from following the sheep to be prince over my people Israel; and I have been with you wherever you went, and have cut off all your enemies before you; and I will make for you a great name, like the name of the great ones of the earth.

—2 Samuel 7:8b-10

Introduction

Luke describes Mary as a girl in trouble, not because of any wrong she has done: rather because she has found favor with God. Sometimes what the world views as trouble and what we find personally disturbing is in fact the work of the Holy Spirit.

When we find favor with God, the Holy Spirit comes upon us and there is birthed in our lives some new creation of God's Spirit. And if we are like Mary we are troubled by it. We want to resist it, but we find the truth of it so overwhelming and so compelling that we can do nothing but say, like Mary, "... let it be to me according to your word."

216

This passage is a great testimony to the power of the Holy Spirit. It is *not* an argument for belief in the "virgin birth." Nor is it an argument against belief in the "virgin birth," although Luke makes it very clear that he believes Jesus to be Joseph's son as well as God's son, because as he points out, Joseph is "… of the house and lineage of David…." Luke would not have written this if he did not believe Jesus to be a blood relative of Joseph. But this issue is not his main concern.

For Luke, belief or unbelief in the "virgin birth" is not the test of genuine Christian faith. There is much evidence to suggest that when Luke uses the word virgin he simply means young girl. The word has quite a different meaning for him than it does for us. But even that is beside the point. As far as Luke is concerned, God could have done it either way. In chapter three, he quotes John the Baptist as saying, "I tell you God can make children for Abraham out of these stones…." If God could do that, God could have sent the Messiah in any number of ways.

To argue for or against the "virgin birth" is to miss Luke's point entirely. For Luke, the test of genuine faith is aquiescence: simple acceptance of the Spirit's presence and will — doing what Mary did. Mary said, "… I am the handmaid of the Lord, let it be done to me according to your word."

This is Luke's main point in chapter one, and it is almost as if he highlights it in large, bold letters; the fact that an old barren woman named Elizabeth should conceive and bear a son, and that the child born of a young unwed girl should be the holy son of God, shows that *nothing*, absolutely nothing, is impossible with God. Such is the power of the Holy Spirit.

Matt David, and his daughter Ruth, learned about the power of the Holy Spirit in a most unexpected way.

Ruth David had always been her father's favorite. It may have been because she was disliked by everyone else, both inside and outside the family. Ruth was big-boned and heavy, ungainly in every way. She had a lumbering gait and a get-out-of-my-way attitude. To have called Ruth boisterous would have been an understatement. She was bossy and rough with children, even though

217

she fancied herself a good babysitter and had once taught Sunday School at the Congregational Church. Ruth was infamous for her screaming tantrums, which occurred whenever she didn't get her own way. She once stopped play at a basketball game because her mother refused to buy her a second soda. The school psychologist said Ruth was slow: developmentally disabled was the official term. Everybody translated that as mentally retarded. It provided an explanation for some of Ruth's behavior, but it didn't help people like her any better.

Ruth dropped out of school in the tenth grade, the same year her mother and father divorced. She went to live with her father in the trailer court on the edge of town. Ruth's mother got the house and the four younger children. Ruth was glad to get away from that part of her family. She had never felt like she belonged with them.

Matt David was glad to take Ruth. He found her behavior difficult, but he was utterly devoted to her. She reminded him of his mother, who had also been known as a disagreeable person. Ruth had her grandmother's sparkling blue eyes and captivating smile, which, though rarely seen, could melt your heart when it appeared.

All went well with Ruth and Matt until just after Ruth's nineteenth birthday. She started running around with older men and staying out all hours of the night. Matt arranged for birth control pills and reminded Ruth to take them, but sometimes she forgot or refused. The inevitable happened in mid-summer. Matt noticed that Ruth appeared to be heavier than usual. He took her to the clinic and the doctor confirmed that she was 4 months pregnant. What was worse, a blood test revealed that she had been infected with the HIV virus. Medications were started immediately, and when the baby was born on Christmas Day he was declared to be free of HIV. The doctors called it a Christmas miracle. It was the first of many signs that this was a most extraordinary baby.

Ruth proved to be a surprisingly good mother. She was tender with her own child, spent all of her time with him and gave him everything a child could need. Matt watched over them, doting on both his grandson and his daughter.

Jacob David, unlike his mother, was exceedingly bright. Matt noticed early on that he developed at a more rapid rate than any of his own children had. Jacob was talking in complete sentences at the age of two and reading before he was five. In kindergarten, he was assigned to the gifted and talented program, and in first grade he was so far ahead of the rest of the class that they had to arrange for a special tutor. The next year he was skipped ahead two grades, and when he was eight he started doing high school level work.

Socially Jacob didn't fare as well. The older boys called him "son of retard" and the B word. There were taunts of, "Your mother is a whore and where is your Daddy?" Jacob often came home with bruises after fights with school yard bullies twice his size. "Hold your head up high," his grandfather told him. "You are a child of God. That is all anyone needs to know."

Ruth succumbed to AIDS on Jacob's ninth birthday. She had been trying to hold on until the party and had supervised the baking of his cake the day before. Matt was devastated. Jacob seemed to take it is stride. He had been preparing himself for years. Jacob had studied the HIV virus, understood what was coming, and explained it all to Ruth in terms she could understand. This was the beginning of what was to become Jacob's life work.

Thirty years later, Professor Jacob Benjamin David helped his eighty-year-old grandfather onto a stage in the faraway city of Oslo, where both of them were presented to the King and Queen of Norway. Dr. David then stepped to the center of the stage to accept the Nobel Prize for medicine. He had discovered a vaccine for inoculation against the AIDS virus.

When it came his turn to speak, Dr. David held up the coveted prize and said, "This is for my mother, Ruth David. I wish she could be here this day to see what God has done."

Author's note:

This story was written on the day that Dr. Jonas Salk died and is dedicated to his memory. Jonas Edward Salk was born in the Bronx, New York, October 28, 1914, the son of a garment worker.

At the age of 40, in 1955, Dr. Salk discovered a safe and effective polio vaccine. In 1952, 58,000 cases of polio were reported in the United States in an epidemic that, in that year, claimed 3,000 lives. Dr. Salk's vaccine was a turning point in the battle against polio. He was at work on a vaccine to prevent AIDS at the time of his death, June 23, 1995.

John 10:11-18

A Wolf In Shepherd's Clothing

"I am the good shepherd. The good shepherd lays down his life for the sheep. The hired hand, who is not the shepherd and does not own the sheep, sees the wolf coming and leaves the sheep and runs away — and the wolf snatches them and scatters them. The hired hand runs away because a hired hand does not care for the sheep. I am the good shepherd. I know my own and my own know me, just as the Father knows me and I know the Father. And I lay down my life for the sheep."

— verses 11-15

Jason Drexler was good with sheep. He enjoyed caring for the sheep on his father's farm. At the age of eight, Jason's father gave him an orphan ewe lamb to raise as his own. Jason bottle-fed her and kept her warm and safe. She grew into a fine, mature ewe, with all of the best features of the Cheviot breed.

When Jason joined 4-H the following year, it was only natural that he chose sheep-raising as his project. He acquired another ewe from his father, had both ewes bred to his father's best ram, and began to raise a flock of his own. Jason's father encouraged him to show his sheep at the County Fair. He taught him how to trim and block the wool so that the sheep's best attributes could be seen by the judges when they were shown. And Jason's father taught him the proper way to handle sheep when showing them in competition: how to set their feet, how to hold their heads up and how to move them from one place to another at the judges' signal. Paying attention to the judge is the most important part of showmanship. Jason became very good at showing his sheep — so good that he took home the showmanship trophy at the age of thirteen. It was Jason's proudest achievement. He didn't have many friends and he wasn't big enough for competitive sports. Seeing his picture with the showmanship trophy on the front page of the newspaper, and knowing his classmates would see it, too, made Jason feel very good about what he had accomplished.

Jason felt very good, too, when the new pastor at their church took an interest in his sheep project and praised him for his achievements. His parents invited Pastor Jim over for lunch one day, and afterwards Jason showed him around the sheep pens, proudly pointing out each ewe and lamb in his own little flock. Pastor Jim said he wanted to learn more about showing sheep, so Jason invited him to come by some time when he was getting ready for a show at the fair.

The pastor stopped in often after that. He soon became a good friend of the family. Pastor Jim helped Jason prepare for the fair and sometimes drove the pickup truck to get supplies when Jason's father was busy. Jason enjoyed the pastor's friendship. Pastor Jim was much younger than Jason's father, and Jason discovered he could talk about things with Pastor Jim that he could not bring himself to discuss with his father. Jason was very proud to have such an important man as Pastor Jim as his friend.

On the day before the fair was to begin, Jason mentioned to Pastor Jim that he planned to stay overnight at the fairgrounds so he could keep an eye on his sheep. He said he always took a sleeping bag and slept in the hay next to the pens. Pastor Jim volunteered to keep Jason company, and so that night the two of them kept vigil beside the sheep. Jason thought it was great fun to have his special friend share in this important event in his life. He couldn't wait for the competition to begin the next day so Pastor Jim could see him showing sheep. Jason was so excited that he found it difficult to go to sleep. When Pastor Jim offered to give him a back rub to help him relax, Jason felt even closer to his special friend. But when Pastor Jim continued the rubbing over more private parts of his body, Jason didn't know what to think. It made him feel very uncomfortable, but Jason decided it must be all right. Pastor Jim would never do anything to hurt him.

Jason put the evening's events out of his mind and did his best to concentrate on showing his sheep the next day. It all went well enough, but things just weren't the same after that. Jason couldn't figure it out; he couldn't get excited about anything, least of all caring for his sheep. Jason tried to talk to Pastor Jim about his feelings. The pastor assured him that he was going through a normal adolescent phase. "It will pass," Pastor Jim said. "Don't worry about it."

A few months later, Jason was helping the pastor put away the communion cups in the sacristy after the Maundy Thursday service, when Pastor Jim again offered to give him a back rub. "You've been looking uptight lately," the pastor said. "You need to relax more." This time Pastor Jim was rough with Jason and made him do unspeakable things that Jason immediately tried to put out of his mind. Again Jason didn't know what to think or do. He told no one what Pastor Jim had done to him.

In the spring of the same year, it was announced that Pastor Jim was leaving the congregation. There were rumors that the pastor had been accused of molesting several children in his previous parish, but no one knew for sure.

Jason was very sad for a long time after Pastor Jim's leaving. One night, after a youth fellowship meeting, his mother found him sitting all alone in the back pew of the church sanctuary. She could tell that he had been crying and she instinctively reached out and put her arms around him. Jason let his mom hold him for a long time. After a while, she said to him, "Did someone hurt you?" Jason nodded. "Was it Pastor Jim?" Again Jason nodded. "It wasn't your fault," Jason heard his mom say through her own tears. "It wasn't your fault. It should never have happened to you."

That was the beginning of Jason's healing. In time, he was able to let go of the trauma of his pastor's abuse, although he would carry some of the emotional scars all of his life. Jason is grown now and has a daughter and son of his own. He is the shepherd of a flock of several hundred Christian souls at a church in the midwest.

Author's note:
Some commentators suggest that the image of the hired hand in this passage may allude to the image of the bad shepherd in Ezekiel 34:1-10, Jeremiah 23:1-3 and Zechariah 11:15-17.

Thus says the Lord God, I am against the shepherds; and I will demand my sheep at their hand, and put a stop to their feeding the sheep; no longer shall the shepherds feed themselves. I will rescue my sheep from their mouths, so that they may not be food for them.

— Ezekiel 34:10

For more information about clergy sexual abuse, contact CASSANDRA, a support group for clergy abuse survivors in Madison and Milwaukee, Wisconsin. Phone 414-257-1228 or 608-251-5126. Write to: The Rape Crisis Center, 128 East Olin Avenue, Madison, Wisconsin 53713.

Jeremiah 23:1-6, Mark 6:30-34, 53-56

Sheep Without A Shepherd

*Woe to the shepherds who destroy and scatter the sheep
of my pasture! says the Lord. Therefore thus says the Lord,
the God of Israel, concerning the shepherds who shepherd
my people: It is you who have scattered my flock, and
have driven them away, and you have not attended to them.
So I will attend to you for your evil doings, says the Lord.
Then I myself will gather the remnant of my flock out of
all the lands where I have driven them, and I will bring
them back to their fold, and they shall be fruitful and
multiply. I will raise up shepherds over them who will
shepherd them, and they shall not fear any longer, or be
dismayed, nor shall any be missing, says the Lord.*
— Jeremiah 23:1-4

*As he went ashore, he saw a great crowd; and he had
compassion for them, because they were like sheep without a shepherd; and he began to teach them many things.*
—Mark 6:34

Christ Community Church was without a pastor for the third
time within four years. Dr. Albert Faithful had died after a long
illness, just before he was to retire from a nineteen-year-long
pastorate. The church had flourished under his leadership and he
was much loved by everyone in the congregation. It was understood
that Pastor Jillian Balm was to be with them on an interim basis for
eighteen months. Many people came to love her in that brief time
and it was difficult to bid her good-bye. But Pastor Balm had done
her work well; the congregation had grieved for Dr. Faithful and
was ready to welcome a new spiritual leader.

The Reverend Elsworth Worthy came to the church with the
highest recommendations from the bishop. He and his family were

warmly received and his ministry with Christ Church got off to a fast start. The Reverend Worthy was a dynamic preacher. Soon the pews were packed every Sunday and a second service had to be added in the chapel. Over a hundred new members joined the church during the first year. A long-time drive to purchase a new organ, which had been slowed after Dr. Faithful's death, was completed and a magnificent new pipe organ installed in the sanctuary. There was talk of building on to the educational wing, for the Sunday School program was also growing by leaps and bounds. Everyone had great praise for Reverend Worthy. "You have awakened a sleeping giant," they told him. They bragged about their new pastor to friends and business associates. "How lucky we are to have him," they said. "You must come and hear him preach some Sunday."

It was near the end of Reverend Worthy's second year when a rumor began to circulate about something going on between the pastor and one of the women in the choir. The leaders on the personnel committee quietly investigated and reported that the pastor had done nothing inappropriate. But the rumor persisted. Factions began to form. The largest group, the adamant supporters of Reverend Worthy, insisted that nothing was wrong, that a few naysayers were trying to destroy the unity of the church. A smaller but very vocal group of long-time members who had expressed opposition to some of the changes Reverend Worthy had made maintained that "where there is smoke there must be fire." But even they were shocked when Reverend Worthy announced from the pulpit on the Sunday before Easter that he was not only leaving the congregation, he was giving up pastoral ministry. The pastor offered no explanation for his sudden decision, but the next day it was revealed that six women from the congregation had filed sexual harrassment charges against the Reverend Worthy. Within a week, several women from two previous congregations served by Reverend Worthy had filed similar charges.

The congregation was devastated. Everyone was shocked. At first many of Reverend Worthy's supporters refused to believe what they had heard. Some blamed the women. Others asserted that the pastor was a victim of the pressures and strains of his position. They implied that the naysaying faction had been responsible for pushing him over the edge. The naysayers tossed the blame right back, complaining that, if certain church leaders had been more vigilant, the whole mess could have been avoided.

The bishop sent another interim pastor, and though well qualified, he was coolly received. Worship attendance plummeted. Many of the newer members left the church. The service in the chapel was discontinued. The building committee, which had recently been formed to draw up plans for the addition to the education wing, was disbanded. The choir director and the secretary resigned. Sunday offerings were so low that the congregation began to default on some of its bills.

The chairperson of the board called an emergency congregational meeting. About ninety of the long-time members were in attendance. Various proposals for actions to heal the congregation were put forth and debated. Some were in favor of calling a new pastor immediately: "Let's put the past behind us and get on with our ministry," they said. "What's done is done, we can't undo it." Others expressed feelings of hopelessness and despair. They didn't see how the congregation could ever recover from the betrayal they had suffered. Some who were quite vocal about their anger said they should hire a lawyer and sue Reverend Worthy, or perhaps the Bishop who recommended him.

The meeting was apparently going to end without an agreement on a plan of action when Ellen Faithful rose to speak. Ellen was the daughter of the late Dr. Faithful and was held in high regard by most members of the congregation. She commented on the deep sadness and hurt they all shared as the result of the weakness of their spiritual leader. "I wish Dad were here," she said. "I am sure he would know what to do." There were many sympathetic and knowing nods all around the room. Everyone became quite still as they waited for Ellen to continue. It was clear that the Spirit had at last found a voice. "Nevertheless," Ellen went on, "we need not despair. We know Christ is with us, and we can be sure that Christ will show us the way out of this unfortunate dilemma."

Ellen's words were followed by a long, deliberative silence. It was the new interim pastor who spoke first, with a suggestion that they all bow in prayer and ask for guidance. After his quiet "amen," the discussion resumed in a new, positive tone. It was suggested that the congregation might hire a consultant to help them express their grief and anger, and give guidance as they explored options for the future. Everyone agreed that this would be a good place to start. The healing of Christ Church had begun.

Author's note:

Congregations in which clergy misconduct has occurred are in need of special care. Nancy Meyers Hopkins observes, in an article entitled "The Congregation is Also a Victim," that "some congregations end up depressed with anger turned inward" (p. 20). She says, "Successors of clergy who act out sexually are at great risk ... of angry projections from their parishioners" (*Clergy Sexual Misconduct: A Systems Perspective*, The Alban Institute, Inc., 1993, p. 6).

David Brubaker tells about the anger and frustration experienced when pastoral misconduct is disclosed: "There may be feelings of abandonment, rage and shock, similar to a family which experiences incest ... They may blame or suspect the victim(s). It is not uncommon for the congregation to be divided into factions as persons try to sort out their own feelings. In one sense the congregation itself has been raped ... Whether or not the congregation can recover depends on its ability to work through the issue with openness and care. An outside consultant, someone trained in conflict resolution or pastoral counseling, can be very helpful. Failure to implement an adequate process can let a situation fester for years and drain a congregation of its spiritual and emotional energy" ("An Intervention Paradigm," *MCS Conciliation Quarterly*, Spring, 1991, p. 9).

See also:

Marie Fortune, *Is Nothing Sacred?: When Sex Invades The Pastoral Relationship* (San Francisco: Harper and Row, 1987).

Lloyd Rediger, *Ministry & Sexuality: Cases, Counseling and Care* (Minneapolis: Fortress Press, 1990).

Anniversary

O Lord, who may abide in your tent? Who may dwell on your holy hill? Those who walk blamelessly, and do what is right, and speak the truth from their heart...

— verses 1-2

Harry and Herman had lived in the big brick house on the hill in Willow Bluff for almost half a century. Some assumed that they were bachelor brothers, but the old-timers will tell you that neither of them are natives. Herman came up from Texas in the late '30s to take over the feed mill when Jim Kinnamen died. Harry was from somewhere out East — Delaware or New Jersey. He worked for Herman in the mill, delivering feed and keeping books, until the war came. They tried to enlist together after Pearl Harbor in '41. Herman was accepted and went on to win the Silver Star in the Battle of the Bulge. Harry had a bad eye, so he stayed home and ran the feed mill for Herman. When Herman came home from the war, near the end of '43, business was booming, and he made Harry a full partner. That was when they bought the old Einerson place up on the hill and moved in together. After a few years, folks just came to accept that neither of them was ever going to marry.

Harry and Herman started going to church in '49, just after the addition was built, when Reverend Swingle was pastor. Harry immediately joined the choir. He had a beautiful tenor voice, and when people found out he could sing he became the soloist of choice at most weddings and funerals. Kate Swarmford used to say that Harry had the voice of an angel, and she made her family promise that when she died they would get Harry to sing "The Lord's Prayer" and "K-K-K-Katie" at her funeral. They kept their promise, and Harry sang both songs just the way she wanted. That was one funeral in Willow Bluff that no one ever forgot. They talk about it to this day.

Herman became active on the church Board of Trustees. He was often seen over at the church, after work and on Saturday mornings, repairing the roof, painting the trim, or puttering with the furnace. When they installed the new pipe organ in '55, the Trustees decided that, while they were at it, they might as well renovate the whole sanctuary. It was Herman who headed up the renovation committee. They made him chairman of the Trustees the following year, a position he was to hold for over thirty years. He had a way of recruiting the right people for a job and organizing them so that things got done in good order.

Their announcement on World Communion Sunday came as a surprise to the congregation and was the source of much puzzlement and consternation in the weeks that followed. Herman stood up during the time for sharing joys and concerns and said, "Harry and I would like to invite everyone to attend our fiftieth anniversary celebration on the nineteenth of November. There will be an announcement in the paper, but we aren't sending any formal invitations. We hope you will all be able to come. We've ordered one of those triple-decker cakes from the bakery, and Harry is planning to sing."

The puzzling began as soon as Herman sat down. "Anniversary of what?" Mildred Hersey whispered to her daughter Gyneth, loud enough for half of the congregation to hear. Gyneth shrugged her shoulders and whispered back, "I don't know." No one seemed to know. When the paper came out that Tuesday with Herman and Harry's picture on the front page, the whole town began to buzz. The announcement simply read, "Herman Fisker and Harry Beechum cordially invite you to attend their fiftieth anniversary celebration on Sunday, November 19, at 2:00 P.M., in the community room at the church."

"I don't understand it," Mildred said to her neighbor, Eunice Criven. "It didn't say fiftieth anniversary of their business or their partnership. You don't suppose they are ...." She couldn't bring herself to finish the sentence. The very thought was abhorrent to her. "To think that they have been carrying on like that here in Willow Bluff for fifty years. I can tell you right now that I'm not going to any anniversary party like that!"

The following Sunday, Herman sat alone in his usual pew in the center of the sanctuary. No one sat near him and no one greeted him before or after the service. Harry sat with the other tenors in the choir loft, and they spoke to him politely, but there was no joking and laughing as there usually was, and no one said a word about the anniversary celebration. It went on like that for several weeks. People began to wonder why Herman and Harry continued coming to church. There was even some talk about formally asking them to withdraw their memberships.

On the Sunday before the anniversary celebration, the organist, Gena Percy, stood up during joys and concerns and asked the pastor if she could say something to the congregation. The pastor nodded and Gena stepped out from behind the organ bench, walked over to the center aisle, and with her hands visibly trembling, began to speak: "I want to thank Herman and Harry for what they have done. It has given me the courage to say something that I have wanted to say for a long time. I am a lesbian. I am not ashamed to tell you that now, even though I know that many of you will not understand. I have struggled with who I am for years and years, and after much prayer, and the support of several dear friends, I have come to accept all that I am as a gift of God. I don't know why God made me this way. I have often wished that it could have been otherwise. There have been times when I have wanted to curse God because of the way I have been treated. But I don't feel that way anymore. I think playing the organ in worship has helped. Praising God with this beautiful instrument is the greatest joy of my life. I thank you all for the privilege of serving God as your church organist."

There was no whispering when Gena returned to the bench behind the organ. No one could remember when the church had been so quiet, except perhaps at funerals. It was a holy silence. Everyone who was present knew that he or she had witnessed something extraordinary, and even though they were all shocked and troubled by what Gena had said, they could not bring themselves to condemn her. To have done so would have been to deny what they clearly saw in her face as she spoke: something holy, something that they had no words to describe, but that they knew was of God. Others would condemn her when word got out that Willow Bluff

231

Community Church had a lesbian organist, but they would not. She was one of their own. They had watched her grow up, seen her baptized and confirmed with their own children and grandchildren; they knew her parents and her grandparents, her aunts and uncles, her brothers and her sister. They were all members of the church, too. Whatever else she was, she was their Gena. Nothing could change that. When one of the newcomers wondered aloud if Gena would be allowed to continue playing the organ, the question was met with a stony silence.

Herman and Harry decorated the community room with crepe paper the following Saturday night. The next day, at 1:45, they stood at the door in their rented tuxedoes, waiting to see if anyone would come. Harry said he was willing to bet his next social security check that they would be eating freezer-burnt anniversary cake for several months. But by 2:15 the room was full and people were still coming. After they had opened their gifts, and Herman had made a little speech thanking every one for coming and saying some of the usual things about what a blessing it was to have so many faithful friends, Harry announced that he had a song he would like to share. He walked over to the piano, where Gena was already seated, and after she played the introduction, he smiled at Herman and began to sing in his sweet tenor voice:

> *For all these years, these friends and these blessings,*
> *we give you all praise mighty God.*
> *For trials, temptations, and hardships endured,*
> *we thank you, O Lord, our salvation.*
> *For this holy union of sinners forgiven,*
> *redeemed, transformed, sanctified;*
> *For grace all sufficient, sustaining, maintaining*
> *our love all these years, thank you, God.*

Author's Note:

The music for "Anniversary" was composed by Kerri Sherwood, Director of Music, First United Methodist Church, Kenosha, Wisconsin. Ms. Sherwood's new CD of original solo piano music, *Released From The Heart*, is available from Sisu music, PO Box 1945, Kenosha, WI 53141.

John 18:33-38

Belonging To The Truth

"For this I was born, and for this I came into the world,
to testify to the truth. Everyone who belongs to the truth
listens to my voice."

— verse 37b

I had a lot of time to think on the long plane ride to Miami. I thought about the phone call from Martin's stepmother. The moment I heard Beata's voice, I knew Martin was dead. He had told me that he was HIV-positive just a few months before. I did not know then how sick he was, and perhaps he didn't either. We were planning to get together when he came home to visit his family. I had looked forward to that visit. I wondered what kind of man he had become. Martin sounded more mature on the phone, filled with self-confidence, proud of the work he was doing, a little world-weary, perhaps, like all of us who have suffered the strains and stresses of mid-life crises, career moves, and the losses of loved ones. But the spark, the effervescent spirit I knew and loved as Marty, was still there. It was hard to accept the fact that, now, I would never see him again.

Martin had told me about the loss of his companion from AIDS two years earlier. Mark had died a lingering, painful death. Martin hoped that his would be quicker and more peaceful. He was planning to retire from his position as Vice President of Patient Care Services at Lower Florida Keys Health Systems in the fall and take a trip to Greece. It was strange to hear one of my contemporaries talk about retirement at the age of 42.

Martin and I had lost touch since he went into the army. There had been only a couple of letters and a few phone calls in 24 years — half a lifetime. And yet I remembered the events of our high school years like they were yesterday. Martin was my first close friend outside of my family. We met in an algebra class. During that year he became my tutor and my best friend. Without his help I may not have passed algebra, and without his friendship my high school years would have been very lonely, indeed — and dull. Martin and I had many knock-down, drag-out, raging debates about politics, philosophy and religion, the nature of existence, evolution, God and Christ. Martin used to write long letters laying out his views on all of these subjects, and more. I was surprised when he finally agreed to come to church and youth fellowship with me. And I was very proud when Martin decided to join the church. He became a liturgist in worship and an officer in the youth fellowship.

In time, Martin began to confide in me about the difficulties of his home life. His parents had divorced when he was quite young. There had been a series of stepfathers after that, and six more siblings. When Martin's older sister went to live with his father in another community, he was given almost total responsibility for caring for his younger brothers and sisters. After a couple of years, it became more than he could bear. He ran away from home and my parents took him in at our farm until the judge could decide who would get custody. With the help of a good lawyer, his father was able to convince the judge that Martin would be better off living with him and his wife. I was sad to see Martin go, because it meant he would be changing schools, but glad that he would now have a more normal family life. We still got together often, but it wasn't the same as seeing each other every day in school.

I wasn't surprised when Martin wrote to me after he got out of the army, and just before he finished his nursing degree at Georgetown, to tell me that he was gay. I had figured that out sometime in the second year of our friendship, when it became apparent that his feelings for me were different from my feelings toward him. I was interested in a certain girl and he was clearly attracted to me. Neither of us let this get in the way of our friendship. We were both honest about our feelings and we respected each other's boundaries.

I'll never forget the night I stayed over at Martin's house, his old home, before he ran away. It was a big deal for both of us. Being a farm kid, with chores to do every night after school, I had never been able to stay over at anyone's house before. Because of the circumstances in his home, Martin had never been allowed to invite anyone to stay overnight. He had the whole evening planned, treasures he wanted to show me, records to play, books to discuss and probably a lot of other things that he didn't get a chance to share. About midway through the evening, a carload of kids from school pulled into the driveway of the house across the street. Martin's neighbor just happened to be the girl I had a crush on. That was one of the bonuses of this first overnight for me. I might get to see her. When the kids in the car and Martin's neighbor invited us to go to the drive-in movie with them, I was thrilled. I wanted to go more than anything else: more than I wanted to spend the evening with Martin. He saw this and was deeply hurt. I felt like a jerk, and, indeed, I had acted like one. I didn't go to the drive-in and I apologized to Martin, but it took us both a while to get over it. The fact that he forgave me is one of the reasons I have always counted him as one of my true friends.

The flight from Milwaukee to Miami went smoothly and the short hop on the commuter jet to Key West was uneventful. I thought about Martin the whole way. There had never been any doubt about attending the memorial service. I put the airline tickets on the credit card and went. It was something I had to do, partly for Martin, but mostly for myself, because I needed to say good-bye. Martin's dad, Bob, and Beata met me at the airport and treated me to lunch at the local Dennys. Later, they would put me up on the couch in a condominium overlooking the Atlantic. The condo had been provided for them by one of Martin's many friends.

We talked non-stop about Martin. They hadn't known Martin had AIDS until about the same time he had told me. Martin's close friends kept urging him to tell them, but he had put it off. Fortunately for Martin and his parents, he had told them in time. They had been with him during a long hospitalization in July, and had arrived in time to be with him when he died.

Martin had died as he wished, peacefully, at home in his own bed, surrounded by his loved ones and Mark's bulldog, Chigger. His friends kept vigil beside his bed for 48 hours. When Bob and Beata arrived Martin was no longer able to speak, but was very much aware of their presence. They were both deeply affected by what happened on the night of his death, by how his many friends tenderly cared for him and stayed with him until the end. Over and over again, during the 24 hours that I was in Key West, I was struck by the great love of Martin's friends. It was a wonderful testimony to the kind of man he had become.

Beata and I stopped at the hospital where Martin worked to see his office and to meet some of the people who had worked with him. As soon as people found out who we were, they treated us like royalty. Everyone had a story to tell about Martin: how the hospital had been made cleaner and safer through his many efforts; how he butted heads with some staff members at first because of his insistence on strict adherence to rules and regulations; and how they came to love him because of all the ways he had loved them. We saw the wing of the hospital that was to be named for Martin. We met people who had worked with him on the Board of AIDS Help Inc. to get more state funding for AIDS patients. We were told about his tireless work with the county agencies responsible for the care of AIDS patients and about his testimony at state legislative hearings. Martin's efforts through the Monroe County AIDS Consortium, which he chaired, had helped to bring hundreds of thousands of dollars to help the poor, the sick, and the dying in South Florida. He had made his life count in so many ways. How proud I was to call him friend.

We arrived about a half-hour early for the memorial service at the Key West Metropolitan Community Church. I sat in the second pew from the front, behind Bob and Beata, Martin's sister Robin, and his close friends, Gina, Gus, Lou and Billy. The pews filled up rapidly behind us. Soon the sanctuary was filled and people were standing in the aisles, along the back wall, and, I would learn later, all the way down the stairs and out onto the street. Many were still in their hospital uniforms. Several members of the Key West Wreckers Motorcycle Club, dressed in full leather regalia, stood like sentries along one of the side walls.

I sat looking at the photographs of Martin on the altar and the flowers from our mutual friend, Tim. I thought about what I might say about Martin if given an opportunity to speak. I kept patting my pocket to make sure the notes I had jotted on the plane were still there. What I hadn't written, and what I had decided not to speak about, was the special bond Martin and Tim and I shared. It was this bond that had caused me to write to Martin just four months before his death.

Martin and Tim and I, and two others, were all sexually assaulted by the pastor of our church when we were teenagers. I wrote to Martin to ask him if he would join me in reporting the assault to the bishop. I told him that I had come to a place in my recovery where it was important for me to ask the church to hold the pastor publicly accountable. Martin wrote back immediately that he would be glad to write to the bishop. It was after receiving his response that I phoned him and we began to renew our friendship. A copy of his letter to the bishop arrived a few days later.

The words Martin wrote on my behalf were running through my mind as I sat there, trying to prepare myself to say good-bye to him:

> *The institution of the church cannot be more important to God than the welfare of its members...*

> *Jesus would have us do everything in our power to protect his flock, his "body" from further violation.*

The memory of Martin's poignant words and his willingness to join me in my quest for justice were a solace in those moments of raw grief. To think that I had invited him into the church ....

My opportunity to speak came early in the service, after the reading of the Gospel, when the pastor invited friends to share thoughts about Martin. I was the first of many who got up to speak. That had to be the urging of the Spirit, because I am not usually so bold. I walked up to the altar and pointed to the flowers Tim had sent. "These are from Martin's best friend in grade school," I said. I shared a few other things that Tim had asked me to say on his behalf, including the fact that both he and Martin had become nurses. Then I introduced myself and told about the Marty I had known in high school, his keen intellect, quick wit, and his delightful sense of the ridiculous. I said:

I always knew that Martin would go on to greatness. As I look on the faces of all of you who loved him, I can see that he did. I shall always treasure the memories of our friendship. I look forward to meeting him again in eternity. I give God thanks for Martin's life. And I pray for a cure for this cursed disease which has taken Martin and so many of our brothers and sisters too soon, too soon.

Author's note:

Martin Clair Elliott was born in Richland Center, Wisconsin, on July 21, 1953. He died September 25, 1995, at his home in Key West, Florida. Martin was admired and respected in all aspects of his life. He was a mentor for those who worked for him and with him. He was an inspiration for persons living with AIDS. During the last year of his life, Martin prepared his friends and family for the final days. Even at the end he took care of others. If there is a hospital or health care system in heaven, there can be no doubt that Martin will be president by the time the rest of us arrive.